JAMESTOWN  EDUCATION

The Outer Edge™
Fateful Journeys

Henry Billings
Melissa Billings

 Glencoe

New York, New York   Columbus, Ohio   Chicago, Illinois   Peoria, Illinois   Woodland Hills, California

Reviewers

Kati Pearson
Reading Specialist/Literacy Coach
Carver Middle School
4500 West Columbia Street
Orlando, FL 32811

Suzanne Zweig
Reading Specialist
Sullivan High School
6631 North Bosworth Avenue
Chicago, IL 60626

Beth Dalton
Reading Consultant
Los Angeles County Office
  of Education
9300 Imperial Avenue
Downey, CA 90240

Carolyn S. Reid
Reading Specialist
Alief Hastings High School
12301 High Star
Houston, TX 77072

 **Glencoe**

The *McGraw-Hill* Companies

Copyright © 2005 The McGraw-Hill Companies, Inc.
All rights reserved. Except as permitted under the United States Copyright Act, no
part of this publication may be reproduced or distributed in any form or by any
means, or stored in a database or retrieval system, without prior written permission
of the publisher.

ISBN: 0-07-872906-8

Send all queries to:
Glencoe/McGraw-Hill
8787 Orion Place
Columbus, OH 43240-4027

1 2 3 4 5 6 7 8 9   024   09 08 07 06 05

Contents

To the Student 1

Sample Lesson: Tragedy in the Air 4

Self-Assessment 12

Unit One

1 In Enemy Hands 14

2 A Dangerous Climb 22

3 Alone Across the Atlantic 30

4 The Last Flight 38

Compare and Contrast Chart 46

Unit Two

5 Holding on for Dear Life 48

6 Courage at Sea 56

7 Out of Control 64

8 Survival at Sea 72

Compare and Contrast Chart 80

Unit Three

9 Escape from Cuba 82

10 Together Again After 50 Years 90

11 Nightmare on a Plane 98

12 Gone in an Instant 106

Compare and Contrast Chart 114

Comprehension and Critical Thinking

Progress Graph 115

Photo Credits 116

To the Student

Every once in a while, people set out on journeys that become life-changing events. They may become trapped on a mountain during a climb. They may board an ill-fated cruise ship. They may try a dangerous escape under life-threatening conditions. There are 13 true stories in this book. In them you will meet people who experience danger on a fateful journey.

As you do the lessons in this book, you will improve your reading skills. This will help you increase your reading comprehension. You also will improve your thinking skills. The lessons include types of questions often found on state and national tests. Working with these questions will help you prepare for tests you may have to take in the future.

How to Use This Book

About the Book. *Fateful Journeys* has three units. Each one has four lessons. Each lesson starts with a true story. The stories are about people who show courage in the face of danger. Each story is followed by a group of seven exercises. They test comprehension and thinking skills. They will help you understand and think about what you read. At the end of the lesson, you can give your personal response. You can also rate how well you understood what you read.

The Sample Lesson The first lesson in the book is a sample. It explains how to complete the questions. It also shows how to score your answers. The correct answers are printed in lighter type. In some cases, the reasons an answer is correct are given. Studying these reasons will help you learn how to think through the questions. You might have questions about how to do the exercises or score them. If so, you should ask those questions now, before you start Unit One.

Working Through Each Lesson. Start each lesson by looking at the photo. Next read the caption. Before you read the story, guess what you think it will be about. Then read the story.

After you finish the story, do the exercises. Study the directions for each exercise. They will tell you how to mark your answers. Do all seven exercises. Then check your work. Your teacher will give you an answer key to do this. Follow the directions after each exercise to find you score. At the end of the lesson, add up your total score. Record that score on the graph on page 115.

At the end of each unit, you will complete a Compare and Contrast Chart. The chart will help you see what some of the stories in that unit have in common. It will also help you explore your own ideas about the events in the stories.

Sample Lesson

Tragedy in the Air

On February 1, 2003, the astronauts on the space shuttle *Columbia* woke up to music. Back in Houston, Texas, Mission Control played them the song "Scotland the Brave." This was to honor Laurel Clark. She was born in Iowa, but her family's background is Scottish. The day before, the music had been Jewish. That had been for Ilan Ramon. He was the astronaut from Israel.

2   After the music, a Mission Control worker spoke up.

3   "Good morning," he called out.

4   "Good morning," Clark said. "We're getting ready for our big day up here. I'm really excited to come back home."

5   Clark could not wait to hug her eight-year-old son, Iain. And she was not the only one who was eager to get home. All seven of the astronauts were excited. They had been in space for 16 days. Now they were heading home. They were due to arrive in a few hours. But it did not work out that way. On this day, their trip turned into a tragedy.

_____

Pictured here are the seven crew members of the space shuttle Columbia.

6   Space travel is dangerous. There are two times when the danger is highest. One time is the takeoff. Luckily, the *Columbia* had gone up smoothly. For two weeks it had circled Earth. Now it was about to come back into Earth's atmosphere. Coming back is the second time of high danger. At this time, a shuttle faces great heat. To protect it, the shuttle is covered with heat tiles. The tiles keep it from burning up. In the past, the tiles had always done their job. "It all happens so smoothly," said one astronaut. "You hardly notice it." In all *Columbia* had made 27 safe flights.

7   After waking up, Clark and the rest of the crew got ready to land. They stored their gear. They climbed into their seats and put on their safety belts. The weather was clear. Things looked perfect for the landing in Florida.

8   At 8:53 A.M., the shuttle crossed the West Coast. It was slowly coming down. Still, it was 60 miles high. At Mission Control, things looked normal. Then a light went out. The light was supposed to show how hot the left wing of the shuttle was getting. At first no one worried. People figured it was just a small problem with the light. Mission Control did not even tell the crew.

9   But moments later, more bad signs came. The shuttle's left tire began to heat up. The pressure in the tire rose. Then more lights went out. Something was

clearly wrong. The left side of the *Columbia* was too hot. Mission Control spoke to the astronauts. "*Columbia,* Houston. We see your tire-pressure message."

10   Rick Husband, the pilot, began to answer. He said, "Roger, uh . . ."

11   Then there was silence.

12   Mission Control waited for more sounds from the shuttle. None came. "That's when we began to know that we had a bad day," said Mission Control worker Milt Heflin later.

13   Other people were sensing the same thing.

14   Out in California, a man named Tony Beasley had gotten up early. He hoped to see the shuttle fly by. Beasley saw a glow as *Columbia* passed through the sky. Then he saw a large flash of light. "It was like a big flare being dropped from the shuttle," he said. He added that it didn't seem right.

15   Indeed, it was not normal. High in the sky, the space shuttle *Columbia* was burning up and breaking apart. Parts of the shuttle fell over three states. Experts think the whole crew died quickly.

16   No one could believe what happened to the shuttle. This was the second time a space shuttle had blown apart. The first time was in 1986. That was when the space shuttle *Challenger* blew up during the launch. All the astronauts on that flight died too.

17   As people mourned the loss, questions were raised. What exactly had happened? The best guess was that the trouble started during the launch. A piece of foam broke loose from the outside of the shuttle. That did not affect the launch. But the foam hit the left wing. It damaged the heat tiles. That meant the shuttle could not safely come back through Earth's atmosphere. "Losing a single tile can do you in," said one expert. One broken tile can weaken all the other tiles.

18   The astronauts had all known the risks. And they had accepted them. They loved their work. Space shuttle astronaut Michael Anderson once said that he had "the perfect job."

19   Kalpan Chawla would have said the same thing. She was the first woman from India to go up in space. "I like airplanes," she once said. "It's that simple."

20   For David Brown, being an astronaut had been a dream come true. One friend said he was "like a kid in a candy store." Someone else once asked Brown, "What if something went wrong?" Brown said not to worry. In that case, he said, "I died doing what I loved."

21   Like the others William McCool loved to fly. Everyone knew that going to space brought that old twinkle to his eye. His sister said, "My brother did what he loved. And he gave his life for it."

A. Finding the Main Idea

One statement below tells the main idea of the article. One statement is too general, or too broad. The other statement explains only part of the article; it is too narrow. Label the statements using the following key:

M—Main Idea   B—Too Broad   N—Too Narrow

__N__ 1. Heat tiles are important to a space shuttle. Without them, heats builds up when a shuttle comes back to Earth. Damage to the heat tiles caused the *Columbia* to burn up. [This statement is true, but it is *too narrow*. It gives only a few facts from the article.]

__M__ 2. The space shuttle *Columbia* burned up and blew apart when it came back to Earth in 2003. All the astronauts on board were killed. The problem was that the shuttle's heat tiles broke during the launch. [This statement is the *main idea*. It tells you what happened, who was hurt, and what caused the problem.]

__B__ 3. Space travel is dangerous. Astronauts become aware of that fact with every fight they take. [This statement is true, but it is *too broad*. It does not tell what happened on the *Columbia*.]

Score 4 points for each correct answer.

_____ **Total Score:** Finding the Main Idea

B. Recalling Facts

How well do you remember the facts in the article? Put an X in the box next to the answer that correctly completes each statement.

1. The space shuttle *Columbia* had been in space for

☒ a. 16 days.
☐ b. 21 days.
☐ c. 45 days.

2. The first sign that something was wrong with the shuttle was

☐ a. a radio that did not work.
☒ b. a light that went out.
☐ c. a tire that blew out.

3. The *Columbia* was the

☐ a. first shuttle to blow up.
☒ b. second shuttle to blow up.
☐ c. third shuttle to blow up.

4. What keeps a shuttle from burning up as it comes back to Earth is

☒ a. its heat tiles.
☐ b. the foam on the outside of the shuttle.
☐ c. the pressure in the shuttle's tires.

Score 4 points for each correct answer.

_____ **Total Score:** Recalling Facts

C. | Making Inferences

When you draw a conclusion that is not directly stated in the text, you are making an inference. Put an X in the box next to the statement that is a correct inference.

1.

☐ a. The astronauts did not think it was possible that something could go wrong.

☐ b. Mission Control does not tell people which day a shuttle is due to come back to Earth.

☒ c. Space shuttles often have small problems that do not cause much trouble.

2.

☐ a. The only times a space shuttle is ever in danger are when it goes up and when it comes down.

☒ b. Heat tiles are less important when the shuttle is going up than they are when it is coming down.

☐ c. The people who planned the shuttle did not know that the heat tiles were important.

Score 4 points for each correct answer.

_____ **Total Score:** Making Inferences

D. | Using Words

Put an X in the box next to the definition below that is closest in meaning to the underlined word.

1. News of the <u>tragedy</u> made everyone cry.

☐ a. funny event

☐ b. exciting event

☒ c. sad event

2. Earth's <u>atmosphere</u> has everything people need to breathe.

☒ a. the air around a planet

☐ b. rocks and soil on a planet

☐ c. plants and animals of a planet

3. Our kitchen floor is covered with wooden <u>tiles</u>.

☒ a. thin pieces of material used to cover a surface

☐ b. hand-carved tree branches

☐ c. bricks

4. The <u>pressure</u> inside this tire was so great that the tire blew apart.

☐ a. a hidden place for keeping things

☒ b. force of something, such as air, pushing

☐ c. a tool that allows things to be seen clearly

5. When Grandpa died, the family <u>mourned</u> for months.

☐ a. sang

☐ b. played

☒ c. was sad

6. We threw out the rug after floodwaters <u>damaged</u> it.

☒ a.   hurt
☐ b.   cooled
☐ c.   kept

Score 4 points for each correct answer.

_____ **Total Score:** Using Words

Put an X in the box next to the correct answer.

1. The author uses the first sentence of the article to

☒ a.   tell the reader when the story took place.
☐ b.   describe what the space shuttle *Columbia* looked like.
☐ c.   let the reader know that something bad was about to happen.

2. What is the author's purpose in writing this article?

☐ a.   to get the reader to become an astronaut
☒ b.   to tell the reader about a trip that ended badly
☐ c.   to describe what happens when heat tiles break

3. From the statements below, choose the one that you believe the author would agree with.

☐ a.   Most astronauts think that sending people up in space is no longer a good idea.
☐ b.   The people who checked the heat tiles before the flight did not do a good job.
☒ c.   There will always be people who want to be astronauts even though it is a dangerous job.

Score 4 points for each correct answer.

_____ **Total Score:** Author's Approach

F. | Summarizing and Paraphrasing

Put an X in the box next to the correct answer.

1. Which summary says all the important things about the article?

   ☐ a. The seven astronauts on the *Columbia* had been in space for days. As they began to land, everything looked good. But then things started going wrong. [This summary leaves out most important details.]

   ☒ b. On February 1, 2003, damaged heat tiles on the space shuttle *Columbia* caused it to burn and break apart during landing. Seven astronauts on board the shuttle died. [This summary says all the most important things.]

   ☐ c. One astronaut on the *Columbia* had a Scottish background. Another was from Israel. Five were men, and two were women. [This summary presents some details from the article but misses too many others.]

2. Which sentence means the same thing as the following sentence? "One friend said David Brown was 'like a kid in a candy store.'"

   ☒ a. A friend said that David had been very happy.

   ☐ b. A friend said that David had eaten too much candy.

   ☐ c. A friend said that David had never really grown up.

   Score 4 points for each correct answer.

   _____ **Total Score:** Summarizing and Paraphrasing

G. | Critical Thinking

Put an X in the box next to the correct answer.

1. Choose the statement below that states an opinion.

   ☒ a. The space program should be stopped before more people die.

   ☐ b. Laurel Clark had an eight-year-old son.

   ☐ c. The space shuttle *Challenger* blew up in 1986.

2. The *Columbia* and *Challenger* are different because

   ☐ a. there was only one astronaut on the *Challenger* and there were seven on the *Columbia*.

   ☐ b. all of the crew members on the *Columbia* died, and no one on the *Challenger* died.

   ☒ c. the *Columbia* blew up on its way down and the *Challenger* blew up on its way up.

3. What was the effect of the damage to the heat tiles on the *Columbia*?

   ☐ a. The astronauts lost control and drove the shuttle into the ocean.

   ☒ b. The shuttle burned up on its way down to Earth.

   ☐ c. All the air went out of the shuttle.

4. Which paragraphs provide information that supports your answer to question 3?

   ☒ a. paragraphs 6 and 17

   ☐ b. paragraphs 8 and 9

   ☐ c. paragraphs 14 and 18

5. How is the *Columbia* tragedy an example of a fateful journey?

☐ a. The astronauts accepted the risks that came with their jobs.

☐ b. The problem with the *Columbia* happened suddenly.

☒ c. The tragedy happened at the end of a trip into space.

Score 4 points for each correct answer.

_____ **Total Score:** Critical Thinking

Enter your score for each activity. Add the scores together. Record your total score on the graph on page 115.

_____ Finding the Main Idea

_____ Recalling Facts

_____ Making Inferences

_____ Using Words

_____ Author's Approach

_____ Summarizing and Paraphrasing

_____ Critical Thinking

_____ **Total Score**

Personal Response

What new question do you have about this article?

_____

_____

[Did anything puzzle you as you read the article? Are you now curious about something the article touched on? Write your question on the lines.]

Self-Assessment

A word or phrase in the article that I do not understand is

_____

_____

[Find one word or a group of words that did not make sense to you.]

Self-Assessment

You can take charge of your own progress. Here are some features to help you focus on your progress in learning reading and thinking skills.

Personal Response and Self-Assessment. These questions help you connect the stories to your life. They help you think about your understanding of what you have read.

Comprehension and Critical Thinking Progress Graph. A graph at the end of the book helps you to keep track of your progress. Check the graph often with your teacher. Together, decide whether you need more work on some skills. What types of skills cause you trouble? Talk with your teacher about ways to work on these.

A sample Progress Graph is shown on the right. The first three lessons have been filled in to show you how to use the graph.

Comprehension and Critical Thinking Progress Graph

Directions: Write your score for each lesson in the box under the number of the lesson. Then put a small X on the line directly above the number of the lesson and across from the score you earned. Chart your progress by drawing a line to connect the Xs.

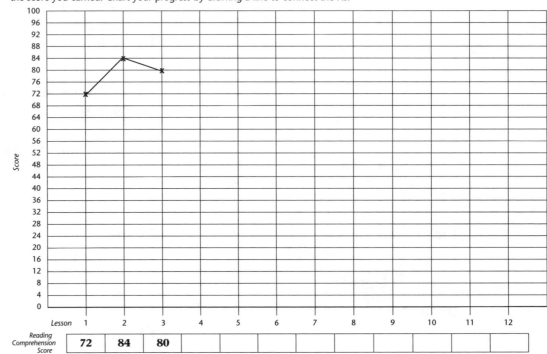

Lesson	1	2	3	4	5	6	7	8	9	10	11	12
Reading Comprehension Score	72	84	80									

UNIT ONE

In Enemy Hands

Shoshana Johnson is carried on a stretcher to a waiting airplane after being rescued by U.S. Marines.

Shoshana Johnson loved to cook. She dreamed of cooking for a living. She hoped to open her own restaurant. That was why she joined the U.S. Army in 1998. She thought the Army could help make her dream come true.

2   For five years, Johnson worked as an Army cook. She picked up new skills. She learned to cook for large numbers of people. Her unit, the 507th Maintenance Company, was stationed at Fort Bliss, Texas. So for five years that was her home.

3   But early in 2003, Johnson's life changed. The United States went to war with Iraq. Johnson's unit was sent to help. It was hard for Johnson to go. She had to leave her two-year-old daughter, Janelle. Still, Johnson was not afraid. The 507th was a support unit. Its job was to help the soldiers who were doing the fighting. Johnson thought she would be in the rear, far from all the action.

4   Things did not work out that way. By March 23, Johnson was in Iraq. It was early in the day. The sun had just come up. Johnson's unit was driving along a road. They were following other units to a new spot. But the other trucks moved quickly. The 507th lost contact with them. Soon Johnson and a few others from the 507th were alone. And then, without warning, the enemy attacked.

5   "It wasn't a little ambush," said James Riley. Riley was another soldier in Johnson's unit. "We were shot from the front, rear, left. It was like being in the middle of a parking lot and everyone is shooting at you."

6   Nine soldiers died in the attack. Johnson managed to dive under her truck. Even so she was shot in both feet. She and her fellow soldiers tried to fight back. But sand clogged their guns. "All our weapons jammed," said Johnson. "And then we just got overwhelmed."

7   There was nothing more they could do. They had to give up.

8   "We had no working weapons," said Riley. "We would have been mowed down."

9   The Iraqis grabbed Johnson and four others. These five were now prisoners of war, or POWs. The Iraqis drove them around in an open truck. The drivers stopped once in a while to show the prisoners to villagers. One Iraqi pulled out a knife. He held it to the throat of POW David Williams. Several other people hit the POWs. Some used their fists. Some used sticks.

10   Johnson and the others were terrified.

11   "It's the unknown," said Johnson. "You don't know what's going to happen to you. I was in a lot of pain. And I was angry too."

12 Patrick Miller thought he might be shot. "That was the first thing I asked when they captured me: 'Are you going to kill me?' They said no. I still didn't believe them."

13 But the POWs were not shot. They were not harmed either. They were blindfolded. They were put in jail cells. And they were asked many questions. But all in all, they were not treated badly. They had two or three meals a day. They often got the same food—rice, chicken, and tea—as their guards.

14 Iraqi doctors took care of Johnson's wounds. She was nervous about having enemy doctors treat her. But she knew she was badly hurt. "I really didn't have a choice," she said. "I knew that I could get an infection and just die. . . . I just had to take my chance."

15 The doctors did a good job. "They did what they could for me," Johnson said. "They even performed an operation. The damage was pretty bad. If they hadn't done that, I wouldn't be here."

16 Meanwhile the war went on. Americans dropped more and more bombs on Iraq. Some bombs came close to the prison where the POWs were. One bomb almost hit them. It blew open the door of their room. But guards kept them from escaping.

17 From then on, Johnson and the other POWs were forced to move from place to place. Every day they were taken to a new spot. No one, it seemed, wanted the burden of caring for them. "We were a hot potato," said Johnson. "It was getting to the point where I believed they were going to kill us."

18 Johnson thought of her family. She thought of her little girl. "My parents would take care of my daughter, I wasn't worried about that at all," she said. Still, she missed them all. And she hoped they would be all right. "I prayed . . . for them to have peace of mind if I didn't make it out."

19 At last, on April 13, Johnson and the others heard knocking outside their prison walls. "I was just sitting there," said Miller. "Next thing I know, the Marines are kicking in the door."

20 "We were so happy to see them," said Johnson.

21 The Marines rushed the POWs to a truck. They drove them to safety. Johnson was filled with relief. Tears of joy ran down her cheeks. "I had to pinch myself a couple of times to make sure it was real," she said.

22 Later, Johnson was asked what she had learned about herself. "You can endure," she said. "I never dreamed that I would have been able to . . . make it through all of this." ✎

A. | Finding the Main Idea

One statement below tells the main idea of the article. One statement is too general, or too broad. The other statement explains only part of the article; it is too narrow. Label the statements using the following key:

M—Main Idea   B—Too Broad   N—Too Narrow

_____ 1. A U.S. soldier sent to Iraq as a cook was shot when Iraqis attacked her unit. After being held by Iraqis for weeks, she was rescued.

_____ 2. Shoshana Johnson was a cook in the army. In March 2003, she was sent to Iraq. She joined the 507th, a unit that does not do much fighting. On March 23, Iraqis attacked her unit.

_____ 3. In a war, no soldier is safe. Even soldiers like Shoshana Johnson, who was a cook, can be shot at or taken by the enemy.

Score 4 points for each correct answer.

_____ **Total Score:** Finding the Main Idea

B. | Recalling Facts

How well do you remember the facts in the article? Put an X in the box next to the answer that correctly completes each statement.

1. Shoshana Johnson's life changed in 2003 when
   ☐ a. her unit was sent to Iraq.
   ☐ b. her daughter, Janelle, was born.
   ☐ c. she got a job as an Army cook.

2. When Iraqis attacked her unit, Johnson
   ☐ a. hurt her back badly.
   ☐ b. was shot in the left arm and the right hand.
   ☐ c. was shot in both feet.

3. Right after they took Johnson's unit, the Iraqis
   ☐ a. sent for doctors to treat the POWs.
   ☐ b. showed the POWs to other Iraqis.
   ☐ c. locked the POWs in a cell and tortured them.

4. The POWs were rescued by the
   ☐ a. Marines.
   ☐ b. Navy.
   ☐ c. Army.

Score 4 points for each correct answer.

_____ **Total Score:** Recalling Facts

C. Making Inferences

When you draw a conclusion that is not directly stated in the text, you are making an inference. Put an X in the box next to the statement that is a correct inference.

1.

☐ a. Shoshana Johnson almost starved after the Iraqis grabbed her and the others.

☐ b. At the time Johnson was grabbed, she knew that she would soon be rescued.

☐ c. Many Iraqi people were very angry at the U.S. soldiers.

2.

☐ a. At times Johnson and the other POWs were in danger of being hurt by U.S. bombs.

☐ b. Johnson will soon forget what happened to her in Iraq.

☐ c. Army cooks do not carry guns, since their job is to support soldiers.

Score 4 points for each correct answer.

_____ **Total Score:** Making Inferences

D. Using Words

Put an X in the box next to the definition below that is closest in meaning to the underlined word.

1. The robbers planned the <u>ambush</u> carefully and started shooting as soon as the train stopped.

☐ a. city meeting

☐ b. birthday party

☐ c. surprise attack

2. Because the pipes were <u>clogged</u> by tree roots, no water could get through them.

☐ a. cleaned up

☐ b. blocked up

☐ c. finished

3. Though they fought hard, the little group of soldiers was soon <u>overwhelmed</u> by the enemy.

☐ a. taken over

☐ b. given a prize

☐ c. left alone

4. Wash that cut well, or you might get an <u>infection</u> in your finger.

☐ a. a beautiful ring

☐ b. a sickness caused by germs

☐ c. an interesting difference

5. Sometimes, caring for my baby brother is a <u>burden</u> I don't really want.

☐ a. family
☐ b. message
☐ c. unpleasant job

6. When bad things happen, strong people <u>endure</u> until good times return.

☐ a. carry on through troubles
☐ b. become a problem
☐ c. make things clearer

Score 4 points for each correct answer.

_____ **Total Score:** Using Words

E. Author's Approach

Put an X in the box next to the correct answer.

1. The main purpose of the first paragraph is to

☐ a. tell about a journey that turned out badly.
☐ b. describe the dishes that Shoshana Johnson liked to cook.
☐ c. explain why Shoshana Johnson joined the U.S. Army.

2. What is the author's purpose in writing this article?

☐ a. to get the reader to join the Army
☐ b. to tell what happened to Shoshana Johnson in Iraq
☐ c. to make the reader feel sad and scared

3. Choose the statement below that best describes the author's opinion in paragraph 15.

☐ a. Johnson should be grateful to the Iraqi doctors who treated her.
☐ b. Iraqi doctors are not quite as good as American doctors.
☐ c. It was a mistake for Johnson to let the Iraqi doctors do an operation on her.

Score 4 points for each correct answer.

_____ **Total Score:** Author's Approach

F. Summarizing and Paraphrasing

Put an X in the box next to the correct answer.

1. Which summary says all the important things about the article?

   ☐ a. Shoshana Johnson always wanted to be a cook. In the Army, she learned how to cook for crowds. In 2003 she was sent to Iraq to feed troops during the war. Her unit was attacked, and she was shot.

   ☐ b. Shoshana Johnson was an Army cook. She was sent to the war in Iraq, where she was shot and taken prisoner. Iraqi doctors treated her well. She was held in a prison for a few weeks and finally rescued.

   ☐ c. Shoshana Johnson was a U.S. soldier in Iraq. Her unit was attacked by Iraqis during the war there in 2003. The Iraqis killed some soldiers and took others prisoner.

2. Which sentence means the same thing as the following sentence? "'We were a hot potato,' said Johnson."

   ☐ a. Johnson said that the POWs were fed hot potatoes.

   ☐ b. Johnson said that the POWs were always too hot.

   ☐ c. Johnson said that no one wanted to keep the POWs for long.

Score 4 points for each correct answer.

_____ **Total Score:** Summarizing and Paraphrasing

G. Critical Thinking

Put an X in the box next to the correct answer.

1. Choose the statement below that states a fact.

   ☐ a. The trucks the 507th was following should not have left the unit behind.

   ☐ b. Shoshana Johnson was the bravest soldier in her unit.

   ☐ c. The Iraqis fed the POWs two or three times each day.

2. Shoshana Johnson and Patrick Miller are alike because

   ☐ a. they were both in the 507th Maintenance Company.

   ☐ b. Iraqi doctors did surgery on both of them.

   ☐ c. they were both shot during the Iraqi ambush.

3. What was the effect when sand got into the 507th's weapons?

   ☐ a. The 507th was left behind the rest of the units.

   ☐ b. The enemy began to fire at the unit.

   ☐ c. The weapons jammed, and the unit had to give up.

4. Which paragraphs provide information that supports your answer to question 3?

   ☐ a. paragraphs 4 and 5

   ☐ b. paragraphs 6, 7, and 8

   ☐ c. paragraphs 9, 10, and 11

5. Which lesson about life does this story teach?

☐ a. You cannot trust your enemy in any way.

☐ b. Each of us is stronger than we know.

☐ c. Every person has perfect control over what happens in his or her life.

Score 4 points for each correct answer.

_____ **Total Score:** Critical Thinking

Enter your score for each activity. Add the scores together. Record your total score on the graph on page 115.

_____ Finding the Main Idea

_____ Recalling Facts

_____ Making Inferences

_____ Using Words

_____ Author's Approach

_____ Summarizing and Paraphrasing

_____ Critical Thinking

_____ **Total Score**

Personal Response

A question I would like Shoshana Johnson to answer is

"_____

_____

_____?"

Self-Assessment

Before reading this article, I already knew _____

_____

_____

A Dangerous Climb

No one had ever made the climb before. Some had tried. But they had failed. Still, Joe Simpson and Simon Yates believed it could be done. They believed they could climb up the West Face of Siula Grande. This 21,000-foot peak is one of the highest mountains in Peru. If the two men conquered it, they would earn a place in history. But if things went badly, one or both of them might die. They both knew that. As Simpson said, "There was no chance of anyone coming to rescue us."

2   In May 1985, Simpson and Yates left their base camp. They hoped to make it to the summit in two days. On the first day, they made good progress. But it was not easy. They had to climb steep walls of ice. They had to watch out for avalanches. Their fingers were freezing. By the end of the day, they were worn out.

3   The next day was even harder. They had to plow through deep snow. They also had to make it past a huge ice cliff. At one point Yates slipped. He and Simpson were roped to each other. So Simpson was able

The peak of Siula Grande, one of the highest mountains in Peru, is seen here wrapped in clouds.

to stop Yates's fall. Still, they came close to being in serious trouble.

4   At last, on the third day, the men made it to the summit. They snapped a few pictures. Then they started back down the mountain.

5   Before they got far, a storm arrived. Snow whirled all around them. The men could not see where they were going. They made their way along the ridge of the mountain, looking for a safe place to descend. Again Yates slipped. But again the rope saved him. When night came, the two men were still high up on the mountain. They dug a snow cave and waited for morning.

6   The next day they started moving again. Suddenly Simpson fell. He didn't go far, but he landed on a hard sheet of ice. He felt terrible pain in his right knee. He knew at once that his leg was badly broken.

7   Fear rose in Simpson's chest. He could no longer walk. He could not put any weight on the leg. There was no way he could climb down the mountain now. Yates would have to leave him and go on alone.

8   But Yates didn't see it that way. He refused to leave his partner to die on the mountain. So he thought of a plan. He would use the rope to lower Simpson straight down the steep face of the mountain.

9   It seemed impossible. But for the next nine hours, that's what Yates did. He sat back in the snow, holding

the rope. Simpson slid down ahead of him. When Simpson got to the end of the rope, he dug in his ice ax. Simpson clung to the cliff while Yates climbed down to him. They repeated these steps again and again. Simpson was in terrible pain. And Yates was worn out. But somehow they kept going.

10 Slowly their hopes rose. Perhaps they would both make it down after all. But then the worst happened. Simpson was sliding down ahead of Yates when he reached a steep cliff. He had no way to stop. He slid over it and dropped straight down. The rope stopped him, but he was left hanging in midair. Below him was a crevasse, or crack in the snow. It was hundreds of feet deep.

11 For almost an hour, Simpson dangled over the crevasse. Above him Yates dug his feet into the snow. He tried not to move. But Simpson's weight was pulling him down. Inch by inch, Yates felt himself slipping down the side of the mountain. Soon he would tumble over the cliff just as Simpson had done. Then they would both fall to their deaths for sure.

12 Yates knew what he had to do—he had no choice. He had to cut the rope. Simpson would fall into the crevasse and die. But at least Yates might live.

13 Finally, Yates pulled out a knife and cut the rope. Simpson plunged out of sight. Without his partner, Yates was able to take a safer route down the mountain. The next day, he made it back to base camp. He knew he had done the right thing. Still, he felt terrible about Simpson's death.

14 As it turned out, though, Simpson was not dead. When Yates cut the rope, Simpson did fall into the crevasse. But he didn't fall to the bottom. He landed on a small ledge of ice inside the crevasse. He had no food and no water. And he was in more pain than ever. But, to his surprise, he was still alive.

15 For hours Simpson lay on the ledge. Then he began to move. Somehow, using just the rope and his ice ax, he managed to crawl down and out of the crevasse. Then he began to scramble down the mountain. He hopped, he slid, and he crawled. It took him three days to cover the six miles to base camp. But at last he made it. He was half dead when he got there. But with Yates to help him, Simpson got well. He and Yates both made it off the mountain alive. They had conquered the Siula Grande.

A. Finding the Main Idea

One statement below tells the main idea of the article. One statement is too general, or too broad. The other statement explains only part of the article; it is too narrow. Label the statements using the following key:

M—Main Idea   **B—Too Broad**   **N—Too Narrow**

_____ 1. Joe Simpson and Simon Yates wanted to climb the West Face of Siula Grande in Peru. No one had ever reached the top of the 21,000-foot mountain before from the West Face.

_____ 2. Mountain climbers know that they may face death on the mountain. When they decide to climb anyway, they accept that risk.

_____ 3. Two men climbed a high mountain in Peru. On the way down, one had to leave the other for dead. Both men finally made it back alive.

Score 4 points for each correct answer.

_____ **Total Score:** Finding the Main Idea

B. Recalling Facts

How well do you remember the facts in the article? Put an X in the box next to the answer that correctly completes each statement.

1. Simpson and Yates made the climb from their base camp to the top of the mountain in

☐ a. two days.
☐ b. three days.
☐ c. nine days.

2. When Simpson fell on a sheet of ice, he

☐ a. got a heart attack.
☐ b. broke his leg.
☐ c. broke his arm.

3. A crevasse is

☐ a. another name for a base camp.
☐ b. a tool used in mountain climbing.
☐ c. a deep crack in the snow.

4. Because Yates knew that both he and Simpson would die unless he did something, he

☐ a. cut the rope and let Simpson fall.
☐ b. crawled back up from the ledge.
☐ c. held onto the rope until help came.

Score 4 points for each correct answer.

_____ **Total Score:** Recalling Facts

C. Making Inferences

When you draw a conclusion that is not directly stated in the text, you are making an inference. Put an X in the box next to the statement that is a correct inference.

1.

☐ a. Climbing the West Face of Siula Grande is pretty easy for most good climbers.

☐ b. If Yates had hung on a little longer, someone would have rescued both climbers.

☐ c. The names of Simpson and Yates can probably be found in a climbing record book.

2.

☐ a. Simpson and Yates never really trusted each other.

☐ b. Both Simpson and Yates had a strong will to live.

☐ c. Yates was not surprised when Simpson got back to base camp alive.

Score 4 points for each correct answer.

_____ **Total Score:** Making Inferences

D. Using Words

Put an X in the box next to the definition below that is closest in meaning to the underlined word.

1. After the army <u>conquered</u> its enemies, it made them lay down their guns.

☐ a. overcame

☐ b. heard

☐ c. followed

2. I pulled myself up to the <u>summit</u> of the mountain and looked at the city below.

☐ a. bottom

☐ b. inside

☐ c. top

3. The <u>avalanche</u> covered the little cabin and broke it apart.

☐ a. a loud sound, like a roll of thunder

☐ b. ice, snow, and rocks that slide down a mountain

☐ c. a smell that comes up from old plants and animals

4. After the climbers got tired of being at the top of the mountain, they began to <u>descend</u>.

☐ a. go up

☐ b. go down

☐ c. go outside

5. She sat by the pool and <u>dangled</u> her feet in the cool water.

☐ a. hung loosely and moved back and forth
☐ b. lifted slowly
☐ c. made an exact copy of

6. The swimmers <u>plunged</u> deep into the water, looking for animals who live at the bottom of the sea.

☐ a. dried off carefully
☐ b. came up slowly
☐ c. moved down quickly

Score 4 points for each correct answer.

_____ **Total Score:** Using Words

E. Author's Approach

Put an X in the box next to the correct answer.

1. The main purpose of the first paragraph is to

☐ a. describe the troubles two men had when they climbed the West Face of Siula Grande.
☐ b. describe what Joe Simpson and Simon Yates looked like.
☐ c. tell how hard the climb up the West Face of Siula Grande would be.

2. From the statements below, choose the one that you believe the author would agree with.

☐ a. Simpson and Yates had some bad luck.
☐ b. Yates didn't try very hard to save Simpson.
☐ c. Simpson and Yates were not good mountain climbers.

3. The author probably wrote this article in order to

☐ a. show why people should not climb mountains.
☐ b. tell the reader a good story.
☐ c. sell ropes and other things climbers need.

Score 4 points for each correct answer.

_____ **Total Score:** Author's Approach

F. Summarizing and Paraphrasing

Put an X in the box next to the correct answer.

1. Which summary says all the important things about the article?

☐ a. Two mountain climbers connected by a rope were coming down a high mountain. One fell off a cliff, and the other had to cut the rope to save himself. He thought his partner had died. It was amazing that both men made it back alive.

☐ b. Climbing the West Face of Siula Grande was harder than two men thought it would be. They had to get through deep snow and ice. But they reached the top.

☐ c. Simon Yates and Joe Simpson were good mountain climbers. They were able to make it to the top of a mountain in Peru. Simpson was hurt on the way down.

2. Which sentence means the same thing as the following sentence? "They had to plow through deep snow."

☐ a. They were forced to plant their feet in deep snow and not move.

☐ b. They had a hard time moving through the deep snow.

☐ c. They needed a plow to get through the deep snow.

Score 4 points for each correct answer.

_____ **Total Score:** Summarizing and Paraphrasing

G. Critical Thinking

Put an X in the box next to the correct answer.

1. Choose the statement below that states an opinion.

☐ a. Siula Grande is in Peru.
☐ b. Siula Grande is the scariest mountain in the world.
☐ c. Siula Grande is about 21,000 feet high.

2. Simpson and Yates are different because

☐ a. only Yates made it back to base camp alive.
☐ b. only Simpson fell into the crevasse.
☐ c. only Yates climbed to the top of the mountain.

3. Yates cut the rope that was keeping Simpson from falling into the crevasse. What was the cause of his action?

☐ a. He thought that if he didn't cut the rope, they both would fall in and die.

☐ b. He was angry with Simpson for causing so much trouble and didn't care if Simpson lived.

☐ c. He knew that Simpson would catch himself on a ledge and would be able to walk back to base camp.

4. Which paragraphs provide information that supports your answer to question 3?

☐ a. paragraphs 7, 8, and 9
☐ b. paragraphs 11, 12, and 13
☐ c. paragraphs 14 and 15

5. How is this climbing trip an example of a fateful journey?

☐ a. The trip took longer than the men had expected.

☐ b. The men tried to work together until they couldn't any longer.

☐ c. The men almost died during the climb.

Score 4 points for each correct answer.

_____ **Total Score:** Critical Thinking

Enter your score for each activity. Add the scores together. Record your total score on the graph on page 115.

_____ Finding the Main Idea

_____ Recalling Facts

_____ Making Inferences

_____ Using Words

_____ Author's Approach

_____ Summarizing and Paraphrasing

_____ Critical Thinking

_____ **Total Score**

Personal Response

How do you think Simpson felt when Yates cut the rope?

_____

_____

Self-Assessment

I can't really understand how _____

_____

_____

Alone Across the Atlantic

1   Debra Veal liked a challenge. And this certainly would be a challenge. She and her husband, Andrew, had agreed to enter the Ward Evans Atlantic Rowing Challenge. This race is held every four years. The goal is simple—to row all the way across the Atlantic Ocean.

2   The race is a test of strength and will. In fact, it is one of the toughest races in the world. Each team consists of two people on a 24-foot boat. The boats have no sails. They have no motors. All they have is oars and a small cabin. The two rowers take turns. One person rows while the other rests. If all goes well, they do this for six weeks. They cover about 3,000 miles. And, with any luck, they live to tell about it.

3   Of the two Veals, Andrew was by far the stronger. He was six feet, five inches tall. Debra was just five feet, five inches tall. Also, Debra had been rowing only a year. Andrew was a famous rower. So everyone thought Andrew would lead the team. But it didn't turn out that way.

Debra Veal raises an oar in Barbados at the end of the Ward Evans Atlantic Rowing Challenge.

4   The race began on October 7, 2001. Things went badly for the Veals almost from the start. Andrew suddenly developed a fear of the open sea. He tried to overcome his fear. But each day it grew stronger. He couldn't help it. No matter how hard he tried, he became more and more afraid.

5   On the eighth day, Debra finished her turn at the oars. It was time for Andrew to row. Debra poked her head into the cabin to wake him up. "I was shocked at what I saw," she said. Andrew was curled up in a ball on the floor. "He was groaning as if in pain." He couldn't even talk. He was consumed by fear.

6   A few hours later, Andrew sadly said, "I can't go on."

7   Debra agreed. "It was the right decision," she said later. "We had to get him off the boat."

8   Five days later Andrew was taken away on a rescue boat. But Debra didn't go with him. She wanted to finish the race. She wanted to keep rowing even if she had to do it alone. At first Andrew tried to talk her out of it. After all, there were 2,650 miles to go. Who would watch for big ships while she slept? What if a storm came and washed her over the side? But her mind was made up. At last even Andrew agreed.

9   Debra was happy. She was happy that her husband was safe. And she was happy about the challenge she was facing. Still, she knew she was taking a big risk. As

the boat with Andrew faded from view, one thought troubled her. "I might never see him again."

10   All alone now, Debra began to row. It was slow going. She had no partner to take over when she got tired. Her fingers grew stiff from gripping the oars so long and so hard. The sun beat down on her. Wind and waves tossed her boat like a toy. The salt spray caused sores to form on her skin. Debra wrote in her diary, "I feel so worn down. . . . I feel so trapped because I know I can't give up."

11   The worst part was being alone. Week after week Debra saw no one. At times she couldn't stand it. One day she sat and cried for three hours.

12   Debra also faced threats from the sea itself. One night a shark circled her boat. The shark was only chasing fish. But Debra thought it might attack the boat. She had seen enough shark movies to think the worst. Debra said that she "hid in the cabin, very scared."

13   Debra could sleep for only a few minutes at a time. She had to be on watch for huge ships. One of them could smash her small boat. And the ship's crew might not even notice it. But one day she stopped watching for a while. She began to clean her boat. She had to—it was a mess. She had thrown some old food over the side. But the wind had blown it back. The food was all over the boat. As Debra cleaned it up, she took her eyes off the sea. She didn't see a big ship moving close. It barely missed her. Debra wrote, "I am at an all-time low. . . . I'm so scared, and I want to go home."

14   Even so, she kept rowing. And she did have some good days. These helped to boost her spirits. She enjoyed watching the sun set. Riding up and down big waves made her smile. And she loved making friends with the sea turtles that swam near her boat.

15   At last, on January 26, 2002, Debra Veal reached land. She had been at sea for three and a half months. In that time, she had rowed all the way across the Atlantic Ocean. She had started in Tenerife on the Canary Islands near the coast of Spain. She had landed in Barbados in the West Indies. Andrew was at the finish line to greet her. He was proud of his wife. And she was happy to see him healthy again. The winning crew had finished 70 days ahead of Debra. But she didn't care. As she stepped onto land, Debra knew that she, too, was a winner.

A. Finding the Main Idea

One statement below tells the main idea of the article. One statement is too general, or too broad. The other statement explains only part of the article; it is too narrow. Label the statements using the following key:

M—Main Idea   B—Too Broad   N—Too Narrow

_____ 1. Some people like challenges. Debra Veal is one of those people, for certain. She proved it on her trip across the Atlantic Ocean.

_____ 2. The Ward Evans Atlantic Rowing Challenge is held every four years. Andrew and Debra Veal entered the race in 2001. They took turns rowing 350 miles. Then a rescue boat had to take Andrew back to land.

_____ 3. A husband-and-wife team entered a rowing race across the ocean. After the husband had to return to land, the wife rowed thousands of miles by herself.

Score 4 points for each correct answer.

_____ **Total Score:** Finding the Main Idea

B. Recalling Facts

How well do you remember the facts in the article? Put an X in the box next to the answer that correctly completes each statement.

1. Every boat in the race had

☐ a. a motor.
☐ b. a sail.
☐ c. a cabin.

2. Andrew had to stop rowing because he

☐ a. got terrible sores on his hands.
☐ b. began to fear the open water.
☐ c. was tired of talking to only Debra.

3. Debra almost let a big ship hit her boat when she

☐ a. was busy cleaning the boat.
☐ b. was looking at a shark circling the boat.
☐ c. was making friends with a sea turtle.

4. Debra finished the race in

☐ a. 70 days.
☐ b. three and a half months.
☐ c. six weeks.

Score 4 points for each correct answer.

_____ **Total Score:** Recalling Facts

C. Making Inferences

When you draw a conclusion that is not directly stated in the text, you are making an inference. Put an X in the box next to the statement that is a correct inference.

1.

☐ a. Most people would have no trouble rowing across the Atlantic Ocean by themselves.

☐ b. Debra was a healthy person.

☐ c. Debra was a person who gave up easily.

2.

☐ a. Tall people are always better rowers than short people.

☐ b. Andrew, members of other teams, and race officials often visited Debra during the race.

☐ c. Andrew probably felt bad that he had to give up.

Score 4 points for each correct answer.

_____ **Total Score:** Making Inferences

D. Using Words

Put an X in the box next to the definition below that is closest in meaning to the underlined word.

1. Climbing the highest mountain in the world is a real <u>challenge</u>.

☐ a. something that is easy to do

☐ b. something that is hard to do

☐ c. something that no one wants to do

2. Every baseball team <u>consists</u> of nine players.

☐ a. is made up

☐ b. is clear about

☐ c. looks into

3. To <u>overcome</u> his fear of snakes, the man forced himself to pick one up.

☐ a. hurry up

☐ b. win out over

☐ c. keep up

4. The old books were <u>consumed</u> by a terrible fire, so no one can ever read them again.

☐ a. made new again

☐ b. set aside or set apart

☐ c. eaten up or ruined

5. Fire can kill plants and animals. It is one of the biggest <u>threats</u> to all life in the forest.

☐ a. forces that make things grow

☐ b. signs of hope for the future

☐ c. things that cause danger

6. To <u>boost</u> her spirits, we brought Grandma a gift.

☐ a. raise

☐ b. close

☐ c. lower

Score 4 points for each correct answer.

_____ **Total Score:** Using Words

E. Author's Approach

Put an X in the box next to the correct answer.

1. The author uses the first sentence of the article to

☐ a. describe Andrew Veal.

☐ b. describe Debra Veal.

☐ c. compare Andrew and Debra Veal.

2. The author probably wrote this article in order to

☐ a. get readers to enter the Ward Evans Atlantic Rowing Challenge.

☐ b. describe creatures that live in the Atlantic Ocean.

☐ c. tell an interesting story about a woman who showed courage on a long trip.

3. The author tells this story mainly by

☐ a. telling about events in time order.

☐ b. comparing different topics.

☐ c. using his or her imagination.

Score 4 points for each correct answer.

_____ **Total Score:** Author's Approach

F. Summarizing and Paraphrasing

Put an X in the box next to the correct answer.

1. Which summary says all the important things about the article?

 ☐ a. In October 2001, Debra and Andrew Veal entered a rowing race across the Atlantic Ocean. Andrew had to give up, and Debra rowed the last 2,650 miles alone.

 ☐ b. Debra Veal often felt sad and tired on her rowing trip across the Atlantic Ocean. But sometimes she enjoyed seeing the beauties of nature.

 ☐ c. Both Andrew and Debra Veal started the Ward Evans Atlantic Rowing Challenge in 2001. But Andrew became so afraid that he could not row or even speak.

2. Which sentence means the same thing as the following sentence? "The race is a test of strength and will."

 ☐ a. Strength and drive make you enter this race so you can test yourself.

 ☐ b. The race pushes you to the limits of your strength and tests your spirit.

 ☐ c. Only strong and willing people are allowed to enter this race and test themselves.

Score 4 points for each correct answer.

_____ **Total Score:** Summarizing and Paraphrasing

G. Critical Thinking

Put an X in the box next to the correct answer.

1. Choose the statement below that states a fact.

 ☐ a. Anyone who tries to row across the ocean alone is taking a foolish risk.

 ☐ b. Andrew was proud of his wife for finishing the trip.

 ☐ c. Andrew probably could have kept rowing if he had just tried a little harder.

2. Debra and Andrew are different because

 ☐ a. Debra was an expert rower but Andrew had not done much rowing before this race.

 ☐ b. Debra was taller than Andrew.

 ☐ c. Debra was able to finish the race but Andrew had to be rescued.

3. One day Debra sat and cried for three hours. What was the cause of her tears?

 ☐ a. She didn't like being alone.

 ☐ b. She had a bad sunburn.

 ☐ c. The salt spray had made sores on her skin.

4. Which paragraph provides information that supports your answer to question 3?

 ☐ a. paragraph 9
 ☐ b. paragraph 11
 ☐ c. paragraph 13

5. Which lesson about life does this story teach?

☐ a. With hard work and a little luck, you can do what you set out to do.

☐ b. It's always easier to do things by yourself than with family or friends.

☐ c. No matter what happens, it's your own fault if your plans don't work out.

Score 4 points for each correct answer.

_____ **Total Score:** Critical Thinking

Enter your score for each activity. Add the scores together. Record your total score on the graph on page 115.

_____ Finding the Main Idea

_____ Recalling Facts

_____ Making Inferences

_____ Using Words

_____ Author's Approach

_____ Summarizing and Paraphrasing

_____ Critical Thinking

_____ **Total Score**

Personal Response

Describe a time when you were proud of yourself for doing a hard job all alone.

_____

_____

_____

Self-Assessment

While reading the article, _____

_____

_____

was the easiest for me.

The Last Flight

Shown here is a baseball photo portrait of Roberto Clemente, superstar of the Pittsburgh Pirates.

As a baseball player, he could do it all. In fact, some people said Roberto Clemente was the best right fielder of all time. He could hit. He could field. And he could throw. He won the National League batting title four times. He won 12 Golden Glove awards. One sports announcer joked, "Clemente could field the ball in New York and throw out a guy in Pennsylvania."

2 But Clemente was more than a great player. He was a great person. He tried to make the world a better place. He thought people should help one another. Otherwise, he said, "You are wasting your time on this earth." His wife, Vera, said, "He would rather be late for a meeting with the governor than pass by a stranger who needed help with a tire."

3 In his free time, Clemente worked with poor children. He taught them to play baseball. He went to see them when they were sick. Once he met a boy who had lost both legs. The boy needed artificial legs. Clemente bought them for him.

4 In December 1972, Clemente took on a new cause. An earthquake had hit Nicaragua. Nicaragua is a country in Central America. The earthquake killed thousands of people. It hurt many more. Hundreds of thousands were left homeless. As soon as Clemente heard the news, he acted. He went on TV. He pleaded for help. "Bring what you can," he said. "Bring medicine. . . . Bring food. . . .

Bring clothes. . . . We need so much. I promise you, whatever you bring we will get there."

5 Clemente was famous in his home, Puerto Rico. When he spoke, people listened. Tons of supplies poured in. People gathered food and blankets. They rushed the supplies to the airport in San Juan, Puerto Rico. Some people also gave money. Within two hours after Clemente spoke on TV, the first relief plane took off for Nicaragua. A second plane followed.

6 But a few days later, Clemente heard bad news. Not all the supplies were reaching the victims. Reports said that the leaders of Nicaragua were stealing some.

7 Clemente was upset. He wanted the victims to get *all* the supplies. He made up his mind to do something. He said that when the next plane took off, he would be on it. "They're not going to steal this load," he told a friend. "I'm going with it."

8 This third plane was leaving on New Year's Eve. No one wanted Clemente to go. Vera tried to talk him out of it. So did friends. They said he should spend New Year's Eve with his wife and kids. Some of them had a bad feeling about the trip. Clemente's own son had a dream about it. In the dream, the boy saw his father's plane crash. "Three times I told my grandmother that Papa's plane was going to crash," the boy later said. "But nobody was listening to a seven-year-old."

9 Clemente, too, had dreamed of his own death. His dream came just a few weeks before the earthquake. He told Vera about it. He said, "I just had the strangest dream. I was sitting up in the clouds, watching my own funeral."

10 In spite of this, Clemente planned to make the trip. He felt he had to go. "If I don't," he said, "who will?"

11 So on December 31, Clemente went to the airport. Vera kissed her husband and said goodbye. Later, she recalled a strange feeling. "I felt a tightness in my chest. Do not ask me to explain it. I cannot."

12 The flight was due to take off at 3 P.M. The plane was old, and it was in poor shape. But it was the best one available. It sat on the runway loaded with eight tons of supplies. The plane was not built to carry that much. But the people of Nicaragua needed it all.

13 As soon as the plane took off, something went wrong. The pilot turned the plane around. He brought it back to the airport. For the next few hours, mechanics worked on it. At last, after 9 P.M., it was set to go again.

14 Once more the small plane took off. But once more the pilot sensed trouble. He started to turn back again.

15 "We are coming back around," he radioed.

16 But it was too late. People later said they saw flames on the left side of the plane. Before the plane finished the turn, it exploded. It crashed into the sea less than two miles from the airport. All five people on board were killed.

17 Roberto Clemente died a hero. Millions cried when they learned of his death. Soon 40 schools were named for him. Major League Baseball honored him too. Other players had to wait five years to enter the Hall of Fame. But in Clemente's case, that rule was put aside. He was voted into the Hall of Fame just three months after he died.

18 Clemente's death was hard for Puerto Ricans. He had been their star. He was the first truly great Latin American ballplayer. He often said that he hoped to be remembered as someone "who gave all he had to give." He certainly met that standard. He gave all he had as a baseball player. And he gave all he had as a human being.

19 Perhaps Vera Clemente put it best. "He died the way he lived," she said. "Nobody told him to go, but he did. That was Roberto."

A. Finding the Main Idea

One statement below tells the main idea of the article. One statement is too general, or too broad. The other statement explains only part of the article; it is too narrow. Label the statements using the following key:

M—Main Idea   B—Too Broad   N—Too Narrow

_____ 1. Some people feel it is not enough to just be good at their jobs. They know that they should also help others who are in need.

_____ 2. Roberto Clemente, a great baseball player, died in a plane crash in 1972. He had been on his way to Nicaragua with supplies for earthquake victims.

_____ 3. Roberto Clemente's family tried to talk him out of going to Nicaragua on December 31, 1972. Clemente got on the old plane anyway. He knew that people needed the eight tons of supplies.

Score 4 points for each correct answer.

_____ **Total Score:** Finding the Main Idea

B. Recalling Facts

How well do you remember the facts in the article? Put an X in the box next to the answer that correctly completes each statement.

1. Robert Clemente came from

☐ a. Puerto Rico.
☐ b. Nicaragua.
☐ c. New York.

2. Roberto Clemente went on TV to ask for help for

☐ a. ballplayers in the United States.
☐ b. his friends in Puerto Rico.
☐ c. victims of an earthquake.

3. Clemente was angry when he heard that

☐ a. his friends did not say thank you.
☐ b. people in Nicaragua were not getting the supplies he sent.
☐ c. no one knew that he had worked so hard for them.

4. Clemente's plane turned around the first time because

☐ a. the plane was not working right.
☐ b. Clemente had changed his mind and wanted to get off.
☐ c. the plane ran out of gas.

Score 4 points for each correct answer.

_____ **Total Score:** Recalling Facts

C. Making Inferences

When you draw a conclusion that is not directly stated in the text, you are making an inference. Put an X in the box next to the statement that is a correct inference.

1.

☐ a. Clemente liked children.

☐ b. Clemente never used his own money to help others.

☐ c. Clemente only helped people he knew well.

2.

☐ a. Clemente always did what his wife and friends asked him to do.

☐ b. Clemente's wife and family could not understand why he wanted to fly to Nicaragua.

☐ c. Clemente put the good of others above his own safety.

Score 4 points for each correct answer.

_____ **Total Score:** Making Inferences

D. Using Words

Put an X in the box next to the definition below that is closest in meaning to the underlined word.

1. The radio <u>announcer</u> shouted, "It's a home run!" and fans all over the city cheered.

☐ a. in sports, a person who teaches players how to play better

☐ b. someone who writes a poem or a short story and then sells it

☐ c. in radio or TV, someone who speaks to listeners

2. The paper flowers look so real that it's hard to tell they are <u>artificial</u>.

☐ a. made by people

☐ b. made by nature and not touched by people

☐ c. beautiful

3. Many of the <u>victims</u> of the flood could not go back to their ruined homes for days.

☐ a. those who are to blame for a happening

☐ b. those who are hurt by an act or event

☐ c. those who tell others about events as they happen

4. We were glad that the motel had one room <u>available</u>, because we were ready for a good night's sleep.

☐ a. able to be used

☐ b. costing too much

☐ c. not able to be found

5. After the <u>mechanics</u> worked on our car, it ran much better.

☐ a. people who plant flowers and take care of gardens
☐ b. people who are trained in selling things
☐ c. people who are good at using or fixing machines

6. To live up to the <u>standard</u> my father set for me, I try to help people in need.

☐ a. kind of coat or jacket
☐ b. example
☐ c. picture of a famous person

Score 4 points for each correct answer.

_____ **Total Score:** Using Words

E. **Author's Approach**

Put an X in the box next to the correct answer.

1. The main purpose of the first paragraph is to

☐ a. tell all the ways that Clemente helped others.
☐ b. show how well Clemente played baseball.
☐ c. tell about Clemente's last flight.

2. What is the author's purpose in writing this article?

☐ a. to get the reader to learn how to play baseball
☐ b. to tell the reader about the dangers of flying in planes
☐ c. to describe the life and death of a good man

3. From the statements below, choose the one that you believe the author would agree with.

☐ a. Roberto Clemente was selfish.
☐ b. No one knew what a good ballplayer Roberto Clemente was.
☐ c. Roberto Clemente made his family proud.

Score 4 points for each correct answer.

_____ **Total Score:** Author's Approach

F. Summarizing and Paraphrasing

Put an X in the box next to the correct answer.

1. Which summary says all the important things about the article?

☐ a. Roberto Clemente was always helping other people. He worked with poor children. When he heard that an earthquake hit Nicaragua, he got supplies together for the victims.

☐ b. Roberto Clemente earned many awards as a baseball player. He won the National League batting title four times. He won 12 Golden Glove awards.

☐ c. Roberto Clemente was a great baseball player and a good man. He died when his plane crashed while taking supplies to earthquake victims.

2. Which sentence means the same thing as the following sentence? "Clemente could field the ball in New York and throw out a guy in Pennsylvania."

☐ a. Clemente played baseball in either New York or Pennsylvania.

☐ b. Clemente could throw a baseball very well.

☐ c. Clemente could run faster than other ballplayers.

Score 4 points for each correct answer.

_____ **Total Score:** Summarizing and Paraphrasing

G. Critical Thinking

Put an X in the box next to the correct answer.

1. Choose the statement below that states an opinion.

☐ a. Roberto Clemente believed that we all should help one another.

☐ b. There will probably never be a ballplayer as good as Roberto Clemente.

☐ c. In 1972 an earthquake hit Nicaragua.

2. From information in the article, you can predict that

☐ a. members of the Hall of Fame will soon vote Clemente out.

☐ b. Nicaragua will never have another earthquake.

☐ c. Puerto Ricans will honor the memory of Roberto Clemente for many years.

3. Roberto Clemente and his son are alike because they

☐ a. dreamed about Clemente's death.

☐ b. decided that Clemente had to go to Nicaragua.

☐ c. helped poor children.

4. Clemente heard that leaders of Nicaragua were taking supplies meant for earthquake victims. What was the effect of that news?

☐ a. Clemente won 12 Golden Glove awards.

☐ b. Clemente went on TV and asked for people to send money and supplies to earthquake victims.

☐ c. Clemente decided that he himself had to take the supplies to Nicaragua.

5. If you were an airplane pilot, how could you use the information in the article to make sure you had a safe flight?

☐ a. I would not travel to Nicaragua from Puerto Rico.

☐ b. I would make sure my plane was working perfectly before I took off.

☐ c. I would never let anyone who is famous travel on my plane.

Score 4 points for each correct answer.

_____ **Total Score:** Critical Thinking

Enter your score for each activity. Add the scores together. Record your total score on the graph on page 115.

_____ Finding the Main Idea

_____ Recalling Facts

_____ Making Inferences

_____ Using Words

_____ Author's Approach

_____ Summarizing and Paraphrasing

_____ Critical Thinking

_____ **Total Score**

Personal Response

I agree with the author because_____

_____

_____

Self-Assessment

One of the things I did best when reading this article was

_____

_____

I believe I did this well because _____

_____

_____

Compare and Contrast

Pick two stories in Unit One that tell about exciting journeys that ended happily.
Use information from the stories to fill in this chart.

Title	Tell about one danger on the journey.	Was anyone hurt? If so, how?	What happened to everyone in the end?

Choose one of the stories. Write a two-sentence TV news headline about it. _____

_____

_____

UNIT TWO

Holding On for Dear Life

The plane was built in Russia. It was not fancy. It was made to carry cargo, not people. But many Africans in Congo fly on this kind of plane anyway. They do not have much choice. They don't have enough money to use real passenger jets. Yet they need to fly. Years of war have left their roads in bad shape. Airplane travel is the only way to get from city to city. Often more than 200 people at a time climb aboard an Ilyushin 76 cargo jet for a flight across the country.

2   There are no seat belts in this type of plane. There aren't even many seats. People sit wherever they find space. Some sit on benches. Some just sit on the floor holding their bags.

3   The Ilyushin 76 does not have a good safety record. Several of these jets have crashed. In fact, nearly 400 people have died in these planes. Worse, airline companies in Congo do not take good care of the airplanes. The planes often look battered and worn. That was true of the plane in Kinshasa on May 8, 2003.

Shown here is an Ilyushin 76 cargo jet similar to the one featured in this story.

Witnesses said it looked "old and run-down." Still, that didn't stop people from getting on the plane.

4   The plane was headed for Lubumbashi, almost 1,000 miles away. There is a large army base there. So the plane was filled with army trucks. Passengers squeezed in around the trucks. Many of the travelers were women with small children. Some women were with their army husbands. Other women planned to join their husbands in Lubumbashi.

5   No one made out a full passenger list. So there was no way to know how many people were on board. Some said it was close to 350. The women and children gathered near the front of the plane. Most of the men sat near the tail. Near them was a cargo door. When it was open, it served as a ramp. That was how the army trucks got into the plane. Workers had driven the trucks up this ramp before the door was closed.

6   After takeoff the plane quickly climbed to 33,000 feet. The weather was clear. It looked like it was going to be a good flight. But there was one sign of trouble. A passenger saw the crew fiddling with the cargo door. He saw them try three times to close it more tightly. The man didn't want to take chances. He looked around for something solid he could hang onto. As it turned out, that move most certainly saved his life.

7 "I was just next to the door and I had the chance to grab onto a ladder just before the door let loose," he said.

8 When the man said the door "let loose," he was not kidding. The entire cargo door blew off. People sitting near the door got sucked out of the plane. The exact number of people who died is not known. Some said it was about 60. Others claimed it was closer to 170.

9 "When the back door opened," said one man, "I fell down and lots of boxes covered me." He added that lots of his friends were sucked out by the wind. "I don't know how many," he said, "because I fainted."

10 "We heard a loud noise inside the plane like hissing," said a third man. "Then the ramp fell off. The airplane swung from side to side. That's when the people fell out. Only the people who had the reflex to reach for ropes on the walls were able to stay inside."

11 "I was asleep and then I heard people screaming," said Prudent Mukalayi. "When I woke up, the pilot told everyone to get to the front of the plane. There were about 40 of us. But people kept dying."

12 Boxes and bags flew around inside the plane. People reached for anything that was tied down. They held onto ropes or netting fixed to the inside of the plane. Holding on was a matter of life and death. If they let go, they would die. They had no choice. No matter how much their arms hurt, they had to hold on.

13 Suzanne Mutelo was on the plane. She had her two teenage children with her. "We were very frightened and held on for all we were worth," Mutelo said. Mutelo saw a woman with a baby get sucked out "into the darkness." She saw a soldier and his young child vanish too. Mutelo and her children knew that the same thing could happen to them if they didn't hang on. So for nearly two hours, they clung to the inside of the plane.

14 The lost cargo door did not cause the plane to crash. The pilot still had control. He turned the plane around and headed back to Kinshasa. There he landed the airplane safely. For Suzanne Mutelo and her children, the horror was over. But the memories lingered. Before she left, Mutelo took one last look around inside the plane. She thought of how crowded it once had been. Now it was almost empty. That was an image she knew she would remember for a long time.

A. Finding the Main Idea

One statement below tells the main idea of the article. One statement is too general, or too broad. The other statement explains only part of the article; it is too narrow. Label the statements using the following key:

M—Main Idea   B—Too Broad   N—Too Narrow

_____ 1. When the door on the Ilyushin 76 blew off, people sitting near it were sucked out. The accident may have killed up to 170 people.

_____ 2. In May 2003, a plane in Congo had a terrible accident. No one expected it to happen. Many people died.

_____ 3. In May 2003 a door blew off on a plane in Congo filled with cargo and people. As many as 170 people were sucked out of the plane and killed before the plane finally landed.

Score 4 points for each correct answer.

_____ **Total Score:** Finding the Main Idea

B. Recalling Facts

How well do you remember the facts in the article? Put an X in the box next to the answer that correctly completes each statement.

1. The plane had no seats with seat belts because

☐ a. all the seat belts had been taken out.
☐ b. people in Congo refused to wear seat belts.
☐ c. it was built to carry cargo.

2. One man became nervous about the plane's safety when he saw that

☐ a. workers were driving army trucks onto the plane.
☐ b. the crew was trying to close the cargo door three times.
☐ c. women and small children were getting onto the plane.

3. The people who were able to stay on the plane were the ones who

☐ a. sat in the back of the plane.
☐ b. sat on the floor holding their bags.
☐ c. held tight to something tied down.

4. When the pilot found out what was happening at the back of the plane, he

☐ a. turned the plane around.
☐ b. closed the cargo door himself.
☐ c. let the passengers come into the cockpit.

Score 4 points for each correct answer.

_____ **Total Score:** Recalling Facts

C. Making Inferences

When you draw a conclusion that is not directly stated in the text, you are making an inference. Put an X in the box next to the statement that is a correct inference.

1.

- ☐ a. The pilot probably landed the plane as quickly as possible after the door blew off.
- ☐ b. Only the weakest and youngest passengers were sucked out of the plane.
- ☐ c. No one thought there was a problem with the cargo door until it flew open.

2.

- ☐ a. Flight attendants probably served good meals on the Ilyushin 76.
- ☐ b. The passengers on the Ilyushin 76 did not have much money.
- ☐ c. Only passengers sitting next to the cargo door were in danger.

Score 4 points for each correct answer.

_____ **Total Score:** Making Inferences

D. Using Words

Put an X in the box next to the definition below that is closest in meaning to the underlined word.

1. Workers loaded sugar, wood, silver, and other <u>cargo</u> onto the ship.

- ☐ a. people who work on a ship or plane
- ☐ b. passengers who come from another country
- ☐ c. things carried in a boat or plane

2. All the <u>witnesses</u> of the car crash remembered different details.

- ☐ a. people who saw something happen
- ☐ b. memories of an important event
- ☐ c. reasons why accidents happen

3. Over and over, the woman <u>claimed</u> to her friends that her dog never bit.

- ☐ a. read in the newspaper
- ☐ b. said that something was a fact
- ☐ c. would not say

4. In the 3-D movie, a bird seems to fly into the theater. Most people put their hands up as a <u>reflex</u>.

- ☐ a. a hat with a wide brim, used in bright sunlight
- ☐ b. a special tool used in making action movies
- ☐ c. an action your body does without time to think

5. The smell of the popcorn <u>lingered</u> even after the snack was eaten.

☐ a. stayed around

☐ b. went away

☐ c. cooked in a pan

6. When Grandpa closed his eyes, he could see an <u>image</u> of his old bedroom.

☐ a. a home

☐ b. a picture

☐ c. a pleasant feeling

Score 4 points for each correct answer.

_____ **Total Score:** Using Words

E. | Author's Approach

Put an X in the box next to the correct answer.

1. The main purpose of the first paragraph is to

☐ a. explain why so many people were aboard a cargo jet.

☐ b. tell why Congo had been at war for years.

☐ c. explain why the Ilyushin 76 was built in Russia.

2. Choose the statement below that best describes the author's opinion in paragraph 14.

☐ a. People should try to forget sad events like this one.

☐ b. The pilot could have done more to prevent the deaths.

☐ c. It was sad that so many died on the flight.

3. The author probably wrote this article in order to

☐ a. introduce the reader to all the passengers on the plane.

☐ b. show how safe most airplanes are.

☐ c. describe a deadly airplane flight.

Score 4 points for each correct answer.

_____ **Total Score:** Author's Approach

F. Summarizing and Paraphrasing

Put an X in the box next to the correct answer.

1. Which summary says all the important things about the article?

☐ a. Passengers aboard a cargo jet in Congo were sucked out when a door blew off. Maybe as many as 170 people died before the plane returned to land.

☐ b. The Ilyushin 76 had been built to carry cargo. It had a bad safety record. Even so, hundreds of people boarded the plane on May 8, 2003.

☐ c. A terrible accident happened in Congo. People held on tight to anything that was tied down when a door blew off. They kept holding on for more than two hours.

2. Which sentence means the same thing as the following sentence? "No one made out a full passenger list."

☐ a. The passengers' names on the list were hard to read.

☐ b. Nobody wrote down the full name of each passenger.

☐ c. Nobody wrote all the passengers' names on a list.

Score 4 points for each correct answer.

_____ **Total Score:** Summarizing and Paraphrasing

G. Critical Thinking

Put an X in the box next to the correct answer.

1. Choose the statement below that states a fact.

☐ a. The Russian builders should have put seat belts for passengers on the plane.

☐ b. Many passengers on the plane were careless.

☐ c. The plane took off from Kinshasa in Congo.

2. From information in the article, you can predict that

☐ a. planes will stop flying between Kinshasa and Lubumbashi.

☐ b. people flying in planes like the Ilyushin 76 will be even more nervous.

☐ c. cargo jets will no longer climb to 33,000 feet.

3. Even if they wanted to, people in Congo can not travel far by car or bus. What is the cause of this problem?

☐ a. War has ruined the roads and made them unsafe.

☐ b. There are no cars or buses in Congo.

☐ c. Most people think that traveling by car or bus is not comfortable enough.

4. How is the flight of the Ilyushin 76 an example of a fateful journey?

☐ a. No one knows how many passengers were on board.

☐ b. The plane quickly returned to Kinshasa.

☐ c. The flight ended in death for many of the passengers.

5. If you were an airline worker, how could you use the information in the article to keep your passengers safe?

☐ a. I would check all doors to make sure they shut tight.

☐ b. I would let passengers sit on the floor in the part of the plane where cargo is stored.

☐ c. I would not bother with seat belts for every passenger.

Score 4 points for each correct answer.

_____ **Total Score:** Critical Thinking

Enter your score for each activity. Add the scores together. Record your total score on the graph on page 115.

_____ Finding the Main Idea

_____ Recalling Facts

_____ Making Inferences

_____ Using Words

_____ Author's Approach

_____ Summarizing and Paraphrasing

_____ Critical Thinking

_____ **Total Score**

Personal Response

I can't believe _____

_____

_____

Self-Assessment

When reading the article, I was having trouble with

_____

_____

_____

Courage at Sea

It's called the Wild Coast. The name fits the place. The waters off the coast of South Africa can be pretty wild. The 361 passengers on the cruise ship *Oceanos* found this out the hard way. On the night of August 3, 1991, high winds pounded the ship. Huge waves crashed against its sides.

2   At first the passengers weren't too worried. After all, they were on a big ship. The *Oceanos* was 492 feet long, and it seemed safe. So that night most of the passengers kept their plans. They went to see the evening show. Then, suddenly, the lights went out. The ship had lost power. Worse, it was taking on water and was sinking. The captain gave the order to "abandon ship."

3   The *Oceanos* had three lifeboats. Quickly, passengers lined up to get into them. They tried to stay calm. They put women and children at the head of the line. But members of the crew panicked. They wanted to get into the lifeboats too. They pushed passengers aside to grab seats for themselves.

This photograph of the ship Oceanos *sinking off the coast of South Africa was named one of the world's photographs of the century by the Associated Press.*

4   After the last lifeboat left, there were still nearly 200 passengers on board. By now it was the middle of the night. No rescue workers could hope to reach the ship until morning. It was too dark, and the sea was too wild. The passengers faced a long, scary night.

5   Waves kept pounding the ship. With no power, the ship grew cold. People huddled in the darkened auditorium. All they could do was wait. They waited for the sun, hoping the *Oceanos* would not sink before morning.

6   Not all of the crew deserted the ship. Robin Boltman stayed. He was the ship's magician. Boltman's job was to make people smile, so he decided to put his skills to work. He did his best to keep spirits up. First he tried singing well-known songs about the sea. But some mentioned dying, so that didn't help. Boltman switched to lively songs often sung in bars. Before long, the passengers joined in. They sang, they laughed, and they even swapped jokes.

7   Boltman then made a quick trip to the ship's store. He grabbed some new shirts and jackets and handed these out to the shivering passengers.

8   At last daylight came. The sea was still rough. The winds were still high. But rescue pilots were ready to go. They flew their helicopters straight into the storm. When they reached the *Oceanos*, everyone felt like

cheering. But relief soon turned to anger. People were shocked to see the ship's captain get into a helicopter ahead of them. The custom of the sea is that the captain should be the last to leave. But Captain Yiannis Avranas ignored this custom. He left the ship with 160 people still on board.

9 Avranas later tried to explain his deed. "I don't care what people say about me," he said. "When I give the order 'abandon ship,' it doesn't matter what time I leave. If some people want to stay, they can stay."

10 His words made the passengers furious. They couldn't forgive him for leaving them. But the captain felt no shame. He just shrugged his shoulders and said, "I have lost my ship. What more can they want?"

11 Back on the ship, Boltman saw that no one was in charge. So he took command. He raced up to the bridge. There he found the radio. He didn't know how it worked. But he managed to figure it out. His first message began with "Good morning, South Africa." Then Boltman stated that the ship was in deep trouble.

12 Helicopters rescued some of the people. Lifeboats sent from nearby ships saved others. Meanwhile, the ship was tilting farther and farther into the water. The passengers knew they had to move quickly. Working as a team, they lifted one another into the helicopters. One man gave his jacket to a woman who had ripped her dress. Some people started sliding into the sea. A woman with a bad hip held out her crutch to them. By grabbing the end of the crutch, these people managed to stay out of the water.

13 Still, a few passengers panicked. They jumped into the ocean. It looked as if they might drown. That's when another hero emerged. Moss Hills was a musician with the ship's band. Like Boltman, he had stayed on the *Oceanos*. Now he climbed into a little rubber boat. He paddled over to the drowning passengers and pulled them into the small boat. Hills managed to get them all to a nearby ship. There they were safely brought aboard.

14 At last all the passengers were off the ship. Boltman made sure the crew was off too. He even thought of the animals. He placed the captain's dog in a lifeboat. The poor thing was so scared it bit Boltman's finger. Boltman's last move as "captain" was to free the ship's birds. He opened their cage so they could fly away. Only then, with all lives saved, did Robin Boltman climb into a waiting helicopter.

15 Less than two hours later, the huge ship sank to the bottom of the sea. "The whole thing seemed like a bad dream," Boltman later said. But thanks to him and Moss Hills, the "bad dream" did not turn into a nightmare. 🎗

A. Finding the Main Idea

One statement below tells the main idea of the article. One statement is too general, or too broad. The other statement explains only part of the article; it is too narrow. Label the statements using the following key:

M—Main Idea   B—Too Broad   N—Too Narrow

_____ 1. Cruises are meant to be fun and relaxing. But the passengers on one cruise ship learned that you cannot count on the sea to be kind. It can also be frightening.

_____ 2. Passengers on the cruise ship *Oceanos* were terrified on the night of August 3, 1991. High winds blew, and huge waves crashed into the ship. The *Oceanos* started taking on water.

_____ 3. The captain and many crew members of a cruise ship left about 200 passengers on the sinking ship. Two brave crew members stayed back and made sure everyone got off safely.

Score 4 points for each correct answer.

_____ **Total Score:** Finding the Main Idea

B. Recalling Facts

How well do you remember the facts in the article? Put an X in the box next to the answer that correctly completes each statement.

1. The captain told everyone to abandon the ship right after

☐ a. strong winds and waves began to pound the ship.
☐ b. the ship started taking on water.
☐ c. members of the crew got into lifeboats.

2. The crew member who sang and told jokes to keep the passengers' spirits up was the

☐ a. magician.
☐ b. captain.
☐ c. musician.

3. When the helicopters came, the captain

☐ a. sent them away because the sea was too rough.
☐ b. helped passengers into them.
☐ c. was one of the first to get on.

4. After everyone got off, the ship sank in less than

☐ a. five minutes.
☐ b. two hours.
☐ c. an hour.

Score 4 points for each correct answer.

_____ **Total Score:** Recalling Facts

C. Making Inferences

When you draw a conclusion that is not directly stated in the text, you are making an inference. Put an X in the box next to the statement that is a correct inference.

1.

☐ a. In a bad storm, most people would feel safer in a tiny boat than in a big ship.

☐ b. Many passengers are grateful to Robin Boltman and Moss Hills.

☐ c. Most of the crew members were polite and kind to the passengers.

2.

☐ a. Robin Boltman was a shy and quiet man.

☐ b. After just a short time, the passengers probably stopped being angry at the captain and crew.

☐ c. The captain cared more about his own safety than about the safety of his passengers.

Score 4 points for each correct answer.

_____ **Total Score:** Making Inferences

D. Using Words

Put an X in the box next to the definition below that is closest in meaning to the underlined word.

1. I will never <u>abandon</u> this puppy. In fact, I will keep it forever.

☐ a. play

☐ b. fear

☐ c. leave

2. The cold skaters <u>huddled</u> close to the fire and tried to warm up.

☐ a. moved far apart

☐ b. got close together

☐ c. blew into the air

3. Nate and Angie <u>swapped</u> lunches. Nate got Angie's chicken salad, and Angie got Nate's ham sandwich.

☐ a. traded

☐ b. shook

☐ c. forgot

4. The police officer gave a ticket to the driver who <u>ignored</u> the stop sign.

☐ a. stood beside

☐ b. paid no attention to

☐ c. finished or completed

5. My sister was <u>furious</u> with me when I left her favorite book out in the rain.

□ a. grateful
□ b. proud and happy
□ c. very angry

6. Luckily, a new leader <u>emerged</u> and helped people solve their problems.

□ a. became known
□ b. went away
□ c. became sicker

Score 4 points for each correct answer.

_____ **Total Score:** Using Words

E. | Author's Approach

Put an X in the box next to the correct answer.

1. The main purpose of the first paragraph is to

□ a. explain why passengers on the *Oceanos* were not worried at first.
□ b. describe a storm off the coast of South Africa.
□ c. tell why the captain did not stay with his ship.

2. Choose the statement below that best describes the author's opinion in paragraph 8.

□ a. The captain should not have abandoned his passengers.
□ b. The passengers expected too much of the captain when they thought he would be last to leave.
□ c. The passengers were cruel not to want the captain to have the same chance for life as they had.

3. The author tells this story mainly by

□ a. retelling events in time order.
□ b. comparing different topics.
□ c. using his or her imagination.

Score 4 points for each correct answer.

_____ **Total Score:** Author's Approach

F. | Summarizing and Paraphrasing

Put an X in the box next to the correct answer.

1. Which summary says all the important things about the article?

☐ a. The captain of the *Oceanos* gave orders to abandon ship. When a rescue helicopter came, he got on and left his ship. About 160 passengers were left behind.

☐ b. Two heroes came forward when the *Oceanos* had trouble at sea. The magician kept people happy. The musician rescued drowning people.

☐ c. The cruise ship *Oceanos* started sinking. The crew and captain left passengers on board. Two crew members were heroes and stayed until everyone was rescued.

2. Which sentence means the same thing as the following sentence? "Only then, with all lives saved, did Robin Boltman climb into a waiting helicopter."

☐ a. After everyone was safe, Robin Boltman got onto the helicopter that was waiting.

☐ b. Robin Boltman saved everyone's life when he climbed into the helicopter.

☐ c. Then Robin Boltman saved all the lives of the people on the helicopter and climbed in.

Score 4 points for each correct answer.

_____ **Total Score:** Summarizing and Paraphrasing

G. | Critical Thinking

Put an X in the box next to the correct answer.

1. Choose the statement below that states an opinion.

☐ a. The passengers helped one another stay out of the water and get onto the helicopters.

☐ b. Robin Boltman took clothes from the ship's store and gave them to the cold passengers.

☐ c. Captain Avranas should be ashamed of himself for leaving his ship before the passengers left.

2. Robin Boltman and Moss Hills are alike because

☐ a. they both stayed behind and helped the passengers.

☐ b. both of them were musicians on the *Oceanos*.

☐ c. neither one of them could figure out how to work the ship's radio.

3. What was the effect of the loss of power on the *Oceanos*?

☐ a. A storm battered the cruise ship.

☐ b. The ship started taking on water.

☐ c. The ship became dark and cold.

4. Which paragraphs provide information that supports your answer to question 3?

☐ a. paragraphs 1, 2, and 3

☐ b. paragraphs 4 and 5

☐ c. paragraphs 2 and 5

5. How is the cruise on the *Oceanos* an example of a fateful journey?

☐ a. The ship sank at the journey's end.

☐ b. Robin Boltman was the ship's magician.

☐ c. The *Oceanos* had 361 passengers.

Score 4 points for each correct answer.

_____ **Total Score:** Critical Thinking

Enter your score for each activity. Add the scores together. Record your total score on the graph on page 115.

_____ Finding the Main Idea

_____ Recalling Facts

_____ Making Inferences

_____ Using Words

_____ Author's Approach

_____ Summarizing and Paraphrasing

_____ Critical Thinking

_____ **Total Score**

Personal Response

How do you think the passengers felt when Robin Boltman gave them the new shirts and jackets from the ship's store?

_____

_____

_____

Self-Assessment

One good question about this article that was not asked would be "_____

_____

_____?"

Out of Control

There were lots of empty seats on the train that morning. Arnouska Zehalko could have sat anywhere. On most days, the 21-year-old office worker climbed to the top level of the train. That gave her a better view. She liked to look out across Australia's countryside. On January 31, 2003, though, Zehalko did not go to the upper level. "For some reason, I went downstairs," she said. It did not seem like a big decision at the time. But it may have saved her life.

2 At 6:57 A.M., the train left the Sutherland station. Zehalko settled back in her seat. There would be a few stops before the train reached Wollongong. So she could relax for a while.

3 Others on the train did the same thing. "I may have been dozing," said Nonee Walsh.

4 Before long, though, some of the passengers sensed trouble. At 7:13 the train passed through the Waterfall station. It headed down a long, steep hill. Here the track cut between high cliffs. It wound around sharp corners.

Shown here are rescue workers at the scene of a train crash 20 miles south of Sydney, Australia.

The speed limit for the corners was 25 miles per hour. But on this morning, the train did not hold to that speed. It began to go faster. Soon it was up to 55 miles per hour.

5 "About two minutes out of Waterfall, we knew something was not right," said Hany Beshay. "I don't know what happened." He added that the train was not traveling at the right speed. He was thinking, "This is not right."

6 Krstana Eftimovski had the same thought. She turned to a friend. She said, "I don't know how we're going to make it alive. We're going too fast."

7 After the corners, the track straightened out. The speed limit rose to 46 miles per hour. But by now the train was moving 70 miles per hour. Ahead lay another sharp turn. The train had to slow down. Otherwise it would never make it around the bend.

8 For 15 long seconds, the train just went faster and faster. It was out of control. As one passenger put it, "It's a horrible feeling to be in a machine which felt like it was not being driven."

9 Later, officials tried to find out why the train had not slowed down. They think perhaps the driver had a heart attack. He may have slumped forward. That would have put all his weight on the lever that controls the speed. In any case, he never hit the brakes. The train barreled into the next turn at full speed.

10   In the second car of the train, Arnouska Zehalko had a perfect view of what was happening. She later said, "I saw the train in front tip, and I knew we'd be next—there was nothing I could do."

11   She was right. The first car jumped off the tracks. It sailed through the air and smashed into the cliff. The three other cars followed right behind it.

12   "I was thrown over the seat in front," said Zehalko. "The pain in my knees was so bad I thought I'd broken them both."

13   "Dust was everywhere," she said. There were "people yelling and screaming and asking for help."

14   As bad as it was for Zehalko, she was one of the fortunate ones. Six passengers were killed in the crash. The driver of the train also died. Most of the dead had been sitting in the upper level of the train.

15   "The train was squashed," Zehalko said, "but I managed to get out. . . . After I got off the train, I stepped over three dead bodies. At first I didn't realize they were dead. I even went to ask them if they were all right."

16   As Zehalko stumbled around, she decided she had to get help. The crash site was far from any homes or buildings. It was way down between steep cliffs. The outside world knew nothing about the crash. Zehalko pulled out her cell phone to call for help, but the phone didn't work. The high cliffs were blocking the signal.

17   "I walked along the tracks slowly with another girl," Zehalko said. At last she came to a place where her cell phone would work. She dialed the emergency number and told what had happened.

18   "We need everyone here," she said.

19   Rescue workers did their best. The first ones to arrive at the crash site had to walk a mile down a dirt path. A terrible sight awaited them. Many people were trapped in the wreckage. Doctors had to crawl past large sheets of twisted metal to reach them. Some people had broken bones. Many were bleeding badly. More than half of the 80 people on the train ended up in the hospital.

20   Christiana Gruenbaum spent 10 weeks in the hospital. Her back was crushed. So was her hand. And she had bad head injuries. For 10 days, she was in a coma. Months later she still had no memory of the crash.

21   "I remember getting onto the train," she said. "I'm glad I don't remember the accident. I hope I never will."

22   But Arnouska Zehalko remembered it. She told one reporter, "Whatever you do, don't compare it to a scene in a movie. It was real, and it was horrible."

A. Finding the Main Idea

One statement below tells the main idea of the article. One statement is too general, or too broad. The other statement explains only part of the article; it is too narrow. Label the statements using the following key:

M—Main Idea   **B—Too Broad**   **N—Too Narrow**

_____ 1. Most people think trains are a safe way to travel. But even trains can have bad accidents. Passengers on a train in Australia know that now.

_____ 2. Passengers on a train in Australia knew something was wrong when the train started speeding. Soon it was going 70 miles per hour down a part of the track where the speed limit was only 46 miles per hour.

_____ 3. A train in Australia went out of control when its driver fell ill. After speeding for miles, the train crashed. Six passengers died, and many were injured.

Score 4 points for each correct answer.

_____ **Total Score:** Finding the Main Idea

B. Recalling Facts

How well do you remember the facts in the article? Put an X in the box next to the answer that correctly completes each statement.

1. Passengers became afraid when

☐ a. the lights on the train began to go off and on.
☐ b. the train started going too fast.
☐ c. another train came toward their train.

2. Most of the people who died had been sitting

☐ a. on the upper level of the train.
☐ b. on the lower level of the train.
☐ c. in the first car of the train.

3. Officials think that the driver

☐ a. decided to crash the train on purpose.
☐ b. was away from his seat for too long.
☐ c. had a heart attack.

4. The outside world learned about the crash when

☐ a. the driver radioed back to his bosses.
☐ b. a passenger phoned the emergency number.
☐ c. a few passengers walked back to the nearest town.

Score 4 points for each correct answer.

_____ **Total Score:** Recalling Facts

C. Making Inferences

When you draw a conclusion that is not directly stated in the text, you are making an inference. Put an X in the box next to the statement that is a correct inference.

1.

☐ a. Arnouska Zehalko knew that something terrible was going to happen as soon as she got on the train.

☐ b. At the time of the crash, cell phones did not work everywhere in Australia.

☐ c. Arnouska Zehalko was probably wearing a seat belt when the train crashed.

2.

☐ a. The train's speed was probably controlled by a computer.

☐ b. Hany Beshay had probably never ridden on any train before that day.

☐ c. At the time of the crash, the driver was probably alone in his car on the train.

Score 4 points for each correct answer.

_____ **Total Score:** Making Inferences

D. Using Words

Put an X in the box next to the definition below that is closest in meaning to the underlined word.

1. Grandpa was <u>dozing</u>, but he woke up when the doorbell rang.

☐ a. reading

☐ b. sleeping

☐ c. singing

2. A girl in the back row <u>slumped</u> to the floor. The teacher rushed to pick her up.

☐ a. fell suddenly

☐ b. whispered softly

☐ c. answered a question

3. The football player <u>barreled</u> across the field with two other players running after him.

☐ a. walked slowly

☐ b. sat very still

☐ c. moved quickly

4. Which <u>lever</u> should I push to open the gate?

☐ a. a bar that is moved to make something work

☐ b. a paper on which directions are printed

☐ c. a sturdy holder for books or magazines

5. The boy felt <u>fortunate</u> when he learned he had won the grand prize.

☐ a. charming
☐ b. foolish
☐ c. lucky

6. After the plane crashed, people studied its <u>wreckage</u> carefully. They picked up each piece and looked for clues about what had gone wrong.

☐ a. messages sent back to the control tower
☐ b. what is left after something is ruined
☐ c. passengers, pilots, and crew

Score 4 points for each correct answer.

_____ **Total Score:** Using Words

E. Author's Approach

Put an X in the box next to the correct answer.

1. The main purpose of the first paragraph is to

☐ a. tell when and where the story takes place.
☐ b. describe the countryside in Australia.
☐ c. explain what happened to the train's driver.

2. What is the author's purpose in writing this article?

☐ a. to get the reader to visit Australia
☐ b. to point out safety problems with trains
☐ c. to tell readers about a terrible journey

3. The author tells this story mainly by

☐ a. comparing different topics.
☐ b. describing what happened in time order.
☐ c. using his or her imagination.

Score 4 points for each correct answer.

_____ **Total Score:** Author's Approach

F. Summarizing and Paraphrasing

Put an X in the box next to the correct answer.

1. Which summary says all the important things about the article?

☐ a. Many people were hurt in a crash in Australia. One woman used a cell phone to call for emergency help. Rescuers came as quickly as possible.

☐ b. On January 31, 2003, passengers on a train in Australia had a bad scare. The train suddenly started speeding down the tracks.

☐ c. The driver of a train may have had a heart attack. His train sped out of control and crashed. Rescuers found six passengers dead and about 40 others badly hurt.

2. Which sentence or sentences mean the same thing as the following sentence? "Most of the dead had been sitting in the upper levels of the train."

☐ a. The upper level was hit hardest. That was where most of the passengers who died had been sitting.

☐ b. Before the crash, most of the passengers sat in the upper level of the train.

☐ c. The train had an upper level and a lower level. Passengers who were dead were all in the upper level.

Score 4 points for each correct answer.

_____ **Total Score:** Summarizing and Paraphrasing

G. Critical Thinking

Put an X in the box next to the correct answer.

1. Choose the statement below that states a fact.

☐ a. Someone should have called the emergency number before the train started speeding.

☐ b. There should always be two drivers for every train, just in case one has a heart attack.

☐ c. The train went about 55 miles per hour where it should have gone only 25 miles per hour.

2. From information in the article, you can predict that

☐ a. Arnouska Zehalko will probably be nervous when she rides another train.

☐ b. the company that runs the trains will not run one on these tracks from now on.

☐ c. no passengers in the world will ever fall asleep on a train again because they will be too frightened.

3. The lower level and the upper level of the train are different because

☐ a. passengers were allowed only on the lower level.
☐ b. more people who died were on the upper level.
☐ c. the lower level gave passengers a better view.

4. What was the effect of the train's great speed?

☐ a. The train cars went off the track.
☐ b. The driver proably had a heart attack.
☐ c. The train went down a long, steep hill.

5. If you were a driver on a train, how could you use the information in the article to make sure your passengers stayed safe?

☐ a. I would ask all the passengers to stay awake at all times.

☐ b. I would make sure another person who could drive the train was near me at all times.

☐ c. I would make sure that rescue workers followed my train everywhere.

Score 4 points for each correct answer.

_____ **Total Score:** Critical Thinking

Enter your score for each activity. Add the scores together. Record your total score on the graph on page 115.

_____ Finding the Main Idea

_____ Recalling Facts

_____ Making Inferences

_____ Using Words

_____ Author's Approach

_____ Summarizing and Paraphrasing

_____ Critical Thinking

_____ **Total Score**

Personal Response

I wonder why _____

_____

_____

Self-Assessment

When reading the article, I was having trouble with

_____

_____

_____

Survival at Sea

Huge waves like the ones in this photo pounded the Cairo III *fishing boat for 22 days.*

Pastor Lopez didn't really like fishing boats. He preferred to stay on land. For most of the year, he worked digging clams in the soft mud along Costa Rica's western shore. But whenever Lopez needed extra money, he went to sea. That's what he did in January 1988. He signed on as a crew member of the *Cairo III*. He knew his family would miss him while he was away. But he needed the income. "Just one more time," he told his four-year-old son. "Then it's back to the clams, I promise."

2 The *Cairo III* set out on January 19. Lopez and four others were on board. They planned to be gone for eight days. But on the fifth day, a big storm struck. High winds kicked up, and huge waves rocked the 29-foot fishing boat. "It's a miracle we didn't go down," Joel Gonzalez said later. "The boat was half filled with water, and we bailed like madmen. We lost our net, the radio went out, and before long the engine overheated and gave out."

3 Day after day the storm raged. The men thought it would never end. At last, after 22 days, the sky cleared. But their troubles were just beginning. With no engine, they could not head back to land. The wind and waves were pushing them farther out into the Pacific Ocean. Said Gerardo Obregon, "We were on our own. It was up to God now . . . and wherever the wind wanted to take us."

4 For a while the men managed quite well. They made a sail out of blankets. They drank rainwater. For food, they killed the sea turtles and sharks that swam near their boat.

5 But as time passed, life on the boat became harder to bear. Every day the problems seemed to grow. The storm had damaged the boat. The *Cairo III* began leaking badly. "We're going to sink unless we bail," Obregon told the men. "And I mean all the time. The leaks are getting worse." The men set up shifts so that two of them were always bailing. Even so, water sloshed constantly in the bottom of the boat.

6 One day sharks attacked them. Half a dozen of the creatures began ramming into the side of the boat. The attack did not last long. But it terrified the men.

7 On another day, a huge whale appeared. It was about 80 feet long. The whale sped toward them with frightening speed. The men were sure it was going to hit them head-on. At the last minute, it dove beneath the boat. The men waited nervously. They had no idea what the whale would do next. One flip of its giant tail could destroy them. At last, after about 20 minutes, the whale swam off without harming them or their boat.

8 By May the men were weak, tired, and sick. Hunger and thirst were wearing them down. Some days they could not catch any fresh food. Often they had no

more than a cup of water each. Jorge Hernandez was tortured by nightmares. Juan Bolivar developed a terrible toothache. Joel Gonzalez wrote a farewell letter to his wife.

9   Through it all, Pastor Lopez tried to keep everyone's spirits up. "Don't worry about death," he said. "Just worry about living." He urged them to keep fighting. He said, "It's possible we're going to die, right? Then let's at least die fighting like men, not like cowards."

10   At last, though, even Lopez felt despair wash over him. It was early June. There had been no rain for a long time. The men were completely out of water. They hadn't had a drop for four days. Now they were dizzy and sick to their stomachs. Their tongues were swollen. Their eyes were becoming glassy. They were too weak even to stand up.

11   Earlier they had agreed that if the end grew near, they would put on their "dying" clothes. By this, they meant their best shorts and T-shirts. They wanted their bodies to look as good as possible if anyone ever found them. So now they put on these clothes. They kept bailing in shifts. But when they weren't bailing, they just lay in the boat waiting to die.

12   Luckily, that night it began to rain. Fresh water brought back the men's strength. They started to feel alive again.

13   At last, on June 15, the men saw a boat in the distance. It was a Japanese fishing boat.

14   "We were all leaping with joy," said Joel Gonzalez. "Tears came to my eyes; I realized I wasn't going to die."

15   After 144 days at sea, the men were safe at last. They had traveled nearly 4,000 miles. And they had set a new world record for staying alive on the ocean.

16   Later, the five men told their story to reporter Ron Arias. Arias wrote a book about their experiences. It is called *Five Against the Sea*. At the end of it, Arias tells what the five men did after their rescue. One became a farmer. One became a truck driver. Only Gerardo Obregon returned to fishing. As for Pastor Lopez, he kept his word to his son. He went back to digging clams. Writes Arias, "He doesn't think he'll ever return to serious ocean-fishing."

A. Finding the Main Idea

One statement below tells the main idea of the article. One statement is too general, or too broad. The other statement explains only part of the article; it is too narrow. Label the statements using the following key:

M—Main Idea   B—Too Broad   N—Too Narrow

_____ 1. When a terrible storm struck, five men and their small fishing boat were blown out into the ocean. The men suffered at sea for months without much water or food. They were finally rescued.

_____ 2. A terrible storm knocked out the radio and the engine on the *Cairo III*. The storm lasted for 22 days. By then the helpless little boat had been blown out into the Pacific Ocean.

_____ 3. A storm at sea can do quite a bit of harm. Anyone on a little boat should feel lucky just to live through one.

Score 4 points for each correct answer.

_____ **Total Score:** Finding the Main Idea

B. Recalling Facts

How well do you remember the facts in the article? Put an X in the box next to the answer that correctly completes each statement.

1. The *Cairo III* started its journey in
   - ☐ a. January.
   - ☐ b. September.
   - ☐ c. June.

2. After the storm ended, two men were always
   - ☐ a. looking for land.
   - ☐ b. bailing water from the boat.
   - ☐ c. yelling "Help!" over and over.

3. The men ate
   - ☐ a. food that they had brought with them.
   - ☐ b. sea turtles and sharks.
   - ☐ c. a huge whale that attacked them.

4. The men were rescued after
   - ☐ a. 35 days.
   - ☐ b. 360 days.
   - ☐ c. 144 days.

Score 4 points for each correct answer.

_____ **Total Score:** Recalling Facts

C. Making Inferences

When you draw a conclusion that is not directly stated in the text, you are making an inference. Put an X in the box next to the statement that is a correct inference.

1.

☐ a. The men were sure they would be rescued someday.

☐ b. The men worked together pretty well.

☐ c. After the big storm ended, the days at sea were always sunny, and the wind was always calm.

2.

☐ a. The time at sea made most of the men want to be sailors from then on.

☐ b. Most of the time, the trip was a lot of fun.

☐ c. The boat drifted to a part of the ocean that not many ships sail through.

Score 4 points for each correct answer.

_____ **Total Score:** Making Inferences

D. Using Words

Put an X in the box next to the definition below that is closest in meaning to the underlined word.

1. Our guide preferred the mountains over any other vacation spot. He hoped to buy a mountain cabin someday.

☐ a. liked better

☐ b. enjoyed less

☐ c. promised

2. With the income she gets from walking her neighbors' dogs, she hopes to buy a bike.

☐ a. things learned

☐ b. fun

☐ c. money earned

3. When I gave my dog a bath, the water sloshed in the tub, and some of it got on the floor.

☐ a. was frozen

☐ b. moved about and splashed

☐ c. stayed very calm and still

4. One terrible storm could destroy these beach houses. The owners would probably just build them again.

☐ a. create

☐ b. offer

☐ c. ruin

5. What those heroes did took courage. No one can call them <u>cowards</u>.

☐ a. people who are not brave
☐ b. people who are very brave
☐ c. people who think before they act

6. The carpenter hit her thumb with a hammer. Now her thumb is so <u>swollen</u> that she can hardly get her gloves on.

☐ a. smaller than usual because of pressure from outside
☐ b. bigger than usual because of pressure from inside
☐ c. having a different color than usual

Score 4 points for each correct answer.

_____ **Total Score:** Using Words

E. Author's Approach

Put an X in the box next to the correct answer.

1. The main purpose of the first paragraph is to

☐ a. describe the western shore of Costa Rica.
☐ b. tell about the terrible storm that hit the *Cairo III*.
☐ c. explain why Pastor Lopez went to sea.

2. From the statements below, choose the one that you believe the author would agree with.

☐ a. It is amazing that all the men lived through the 144 days at sea.
☐ b. The biggest danger the men faced was a shark attack.
☐ c. The men should not have killed sea turtles since these animals are dying out.

3. The author probably wrote this article in order to

☐ a. tell a story of how men survived at sea.
☐ b. make the reader afraid of the ocean.
☐ c. describe the animals that live in the ocean.

Score 4 points for each correct answer.

_____ **Total Score:** Author's Approach

F. Summarizing and Paraphrasing

Put an X in the box next to the correct answer.

1. Which summary says all the important things about the article?

   ☐ a. Pastor Lopez was one of the members of the crew of a small fishing boat. He had told his son that this would be his last fishing trip. He preferred digging for clams.

   ☐ b. A fishing trip off Costa Rica that should have lasted eight days instead lasted 144 days. A small boat ran into a storm and was blown out to sea. The five men aboard survived and were rescued by a passing boat.

   ☐ c. Five men on a boat in the Pacific Ocean faced many dangers. They were attacked by sharks. Once, a huge whale swam at them at full speed. They lived through hunger and thirst.

2. Which sentence means the same thing as the following sentence? "At last, though, even Lopez felt despair wash over him."

   ☐ a. Finally, even Lopez started feeling hopeless.

   ☐ b. Finally, though, Lopez decided to take a bath.

   ☐ c. At the end, Lopez was sad to feel the ocean water splashing on him.

Score 4 points for each correct answer.

_____ **Total Score:** Summarizing and Paraphrasing

G. Critical Thinking

Put an X in the box next to the correct answer.

1. Choose the statement below that states a fact.

   ☐ a. The crew of the *Cairo III* should have taken a second radio on their trip.

   ☐ b. The crew of the little boat complained too much.

   ☐ c. The men set a record for surviving at sea for the longest time.

2. From information in the article, you can predict that

   ☐ a. Lopez will never be part of a fishing boat crew again.

   ☐ b. Lopez will never need extra income again.

   ☐ c. Lopez's son will be a fisherman when he grows up.

3. At one time, the men had given up hope and were just waiting to die. But something happened that made them feel better. What was the cause of this change?

   ☐ a. A rain shower gave them fresh water to drink.

   ☐ b. Lopez lifted their spirits with his hopeful words.

   ☐ c. Dressing in their best clothes made them feel better.

4. Which paragraphs provide information that supports your answer to question 3?

   ☐ a. paragraphs 5, 6, and 7

   ☐ b. paragraphs 11 and 12

   ☐ c. paragraphs 9 and 10

5. How is this fishing trip of the *Cairo III* an example of a fateful journey?

☐ a. The fishermen on the trip ate seafood that they caught, and they drank rainwater.

☐ b. The trip was much longer and harder than expected.

☐ c. Five men went on the trip.

Score 4 points for each correct answer.

_____ **Total Score:** Critical Thinking

Enter your score for each activity. Add the scores together. Record your total score on the graph on page 115.

_____ Finding the Main Idea

_____ Recalling Facts

_____ Making Inferences

_____ Using Words

_____ Author's Approach

_____ Summarizing and Paraphrasing

_____ Critical Thinking

_____ **Total Score**

Personal Response

What was most surprising or interesting to you about this article? _____

_____

_____

Self-Assessment

From reading this article, I have learned _____

_____

_____

Compare and Contrast

Pick two stories in Unit Two that tell how a journey became dangerous.
Use information from the stories to fill in this chart.

Title	What means of travel did the travelers use?	What happened to make the journey dangerous?	What problems did the travelers experience?

If you had to be on one of the journeys, which would you like less? Explain why. _____

_____

_____

UNIT THREE

Escape from Cuba

Elian Gonzalez is shown with his cousin aftering arriving in Miami from Cuba.

They had to keep it secret. If anyone found out, they would all be in trouble. Twenty-nine-year-old Elizabet Brotons didn't even dare tell her parents. She just said she was going out for the day. But, in fact, Elizabet and 14 others were planning to leave the country. They were planning to sneak out of Cuba and make their way to the United States.

2 Every year hundreds of Cubans try to make this trip. They don't like living in a communist country. They long for the freedom of life in the United States. So they pile into old boats or homemade rafts and set out for Florida. It is only a 90-mile trip. But their boats leak. Their rafts sink. Storms come up. The Cuban police spot them. And so many of these refugees never reach Florida.

3 Elizabet knew the risks. But she wanted a better life for herself and her six-year-old son, Elian Gonzalez. Her new husband, Lazaro Munero, promised he could lead them safely to the United States. So on Saturday, November 21, 1999, Elizabet got up before dawn. She and Lazaro took Elian down to the shore. There they met the 12 people who were going with them.

4 The travelers climbed into Lazaro's 17-foot metal boat. He had built it himself from spare parts. He had even built the motor. He was sure it could handle the trip. But just to be safe, he tied a couple of inner tubes behind it. These could be used as life rafts in an emergency.

5 The group set out at 4:30 A.M. They did not get very far. The boat's motor died after only a mile. Lazaro and his passengers had to row back to shore. Lazaro promised to have the motor fixed in a few hours. He told everyone to come back the next day.

6 On Sunday morning the group gathered again. By then one young woman had grown nervous. She thought the trip might be too difficult for her five-year-old daughter. So this time she left the little girl behind.

7 It was barely dawn when the group set out. The hours passed slowly. As people got hungry, they ate the food Lazaro had packed for them, including bread, cheese, hot dogs, and fresh water.

8 The group hoped to be in Florida by night, but when the sun set, they were still at sea. That night a storm moved in, and the water became very rough. To make matters worse, the boat's motor quit. Now the group was at the mercy of the ocean. Five-foot waves rocked them wildly. Some of the water spilled into the bottom of the boat. The frightened passengers began to bail. All through the night they scooped out water to keep the boat from sinking. The next day was no better. By Tuesday night everyone was exhausted. And just when it seemed that things could not get worse, a wave caught the boat and tipped it over.

9 Lazaro and the others managed to turn the boat right side up. But now it had a lot of water in it. They feared it would sink if they climbed aboard. So they grabbed the inner tubes and hung onto those.

10 When Wednesday dawned, the travelers were in bad shape. They were tired, hungry, and thirsty. And they were drifting aimlessly through the choppy water. One by one, they began to give up hope. Lazaro was the first to go. Until this time, he had been the group's leader. But he had no idea how to get them out of this mess. After hanging onto the inner tube for a while, he simply let go. He slipped away into the sea, never to be seen again.

11 Over the next few hours, other passengers did the same thing. Those who still clung to life were growing weaker. Elizabet feared that Elian, too, would drop into the water. So she tied him onto an inner tube. Soon after that, she ran out of strength. She disappeared under the waves just as the others had done.

12 At last, only three travelers were left. A man and woman clung to one of the inner tubes. Elian remained tied to the other one. Sometime that night, the rope connecting the two inner tubes came loose. By the next morning, the two tubes had drifted far apart. Now Elian was truly alone. But it didn't matter to him. He was too weak to care. He just lay there mumbling a simple prayer.

13 Elian did not know it, but he was now just three miles from the Florida coast. That morning, two Florida fishermen spotted him. They saw the inner tube with Elian on top of it. At first they thought he was a doll. Then they saw him raise one hand and wave feebly.

14 Quickly, the fishermen made their way to Elian. They pulled him into their boat. They hugged him and kissed him and let him fall asleep in their arms. "He never showed any tears or signs of being scared," one of the fishermen later said.

15 Indeed, Elian's ordeal had been terrible. Only he and the two adults on the other inner tube had survived.

A. Finding the Main Idea

One statement below tells the main idea of the article. One statement is too general, or too broad. The other statement explains only part of the article; it is too narrow. Label the statements using the following key:

M—Main Idea   B—Too Broad   N—Too Narrow

_____ 1. Fifteen people escaping from Cuba headed for Florida in a small boat. Sadly, most of them drowned on the way. Only two adults and one little boy survived.

_____ 2. Elizabet Brotons; her son, Elian Gonzalez; her husband, Lazaro; and 12 others set out from Cuba in November 1999 in a small boat. A short time later, the boat tipped over.

_____ 3. A group of travelers from Cuba took a trip to Florida. Bad luck and bad weather turned their trip into a terrible nightmare.

Score 4 points for each correct answer.

_____ **Total Score:** Finding the Main Idea

B. Recalling Facts

How well do you remember the facts in the article? Put an X in the box next to the answer that correctly completes each statement.

1. Cuba and Florida are
☐ a. 10 miles apart.
☐ b. 90 miles apart.
☐ c. 300 miles apart.

2. Some Cubans leave their homes and go to the United States because
☐ a. they think the weather will be better.
☐ b. Cuban leaders have asked people to leave.
☐ c. they believe they will have freedom.

3. After the boat tipped over, the group held onto
☐ a. inner tubes.
☐ b. the sides of the boat.
☐ c. life jackets.

4. Elian Gonzalez was found by
☐ a. the Coast Guard.
☐ b. two Florida fishermen.
☐ c. other Cuban refugees.

Score 4 points for each correct answer.

_____ **Total Score:** Recalling Facts

C. Making Inferences

When you draw a conclusion that is not directly stated in the text, you are making an inference. Put an X in the box next to the statement that is a correct inference.

1.

☐ a. Lazaro was not a rich man.

☐ b. Lazaro's group brought everything they would need in the United States with them, including furniture and suitcases.

☐ c. No one else on the small boat trusted Lazaro at all.

2.

☐ a. Lazaro and Elizabet knew that a terrible storm was on its way when they began their trip.

☐ b. Elizabet wanted to get to the United States very badly.

☐ c. Holding onto an inner tube for hours is easy.

Score 4 points for each correct answer.

_____ **Total Score:** Making Inferences

D. Using Words

Put an X in the box next to the definition below that is closest in meaning to the underlined word.

1. Our club is looking for new homes for <u>refugees</u> from that country.

☐ a. people who want to join a school or club

☐ b. people who escaped from their home country

☐ c. people who have been in prison or jail

2. After cleaning the house from attic to basement, the family was <u>exhausted</u>.

☐ a. very tired

☐ b. healthy

☐ c. nervous

3. The small boat turned upside down in the <u>choppy</u> lake.

☐ a. calm, with no waves

☐ b. rough, with short waves

☐ c. beautiful, with blue-green water

4. He wandered <u>aimlessly</u> around the house, not knowing what to do with himself.

☐ a. quickly and surely

☐ b. in an angry way

☐ c. without a clear goal

5. The worried mother could barely hear her sick son coughing <u>feebly</u>.

☐ a. as a joke or for fun
☐ b. loudly and strongly
☐ c. in a weak way

6. The families who survived the flood tried to forget their <u>ordeal</u>.

☐ a. a painful experience
☐ b. a pleasant event
☐ c. map of an area

Score 4 points for each correct answer.

_____ **Total Score:** Using Words

E. **Author's Approach**

Put an X in the box next to the correct answer.

1. What is the author's purpose in writing this article?

☐ a. to get the reader to use a life jacket in a boat
☐ b. to tell the reader about a boy who survived a dangerous trip
☐ c. to describe what happens when people don't follow the rules

2. From the statements below, choose the one that you believe the author would agree with.

☐ a. The men who found Elian expected to see a young boy alone on an inner tube in the ocean.
☐ b. All along, Lazaro and Elizabet thought there was no chance that they would ever get to Florida.
☐ c. Elian Gonzalez's life was forever changed by what happened on the trip.

3. Choose the statement below that is the weakest argument against trying to escape from Cuba on a small boat.

☐ a. You might die on the way.
☐ b. You might run into some bad weather.
☐ c. You might get a bad sunburn on the way.

Score 4 points for each correct answer.

_____ **Total Score:** Author's Approach

F. Summarizing and Paraphrasing

Put an X in the box next to the correct answer.

1. Which summary says all the important things about the article?

   ☐ a. At dawn on November 22, 1999, a group of Cuban refugees set out for Florida and a new life. Among them were Elizabet Brotons; her husband, Lazaro Munero; and her son, Elian Gonzalez. They used a homemade boat.

   ☐ b. In November 1999, 15 Cubans tried to escape to Florida in a small boat. Soon a huge wave threw everyone into the water. Only three people survived, including a boy who was tied to an inner tube.

   ☐ c. A group of 15 Cubans thought they would reach Florida in one day. Instead, a storm hit, and then the boat's motor died. A huge wave came along, and the group clung to inner tubes for hours.

2. Which sentence means the same thing as the following sentence? "Now the group was at the mercy of the ocean."

   ☐ a. Now the ocean became kinder to the group.
   ☐ b. The group thought that the ocean was full of kindness.
   ☐ c. The ocean, not the group, was now in charge.

Score 4 points for each correct answer.

_____ **Total Score:** Summarizing and Paraphrasing

G. Critical Thinking

Put an X in the box next to the correct answer.

1. Choose the statement below that states an opinion.

   ☐ a. The fishermen who found Elian were kinder than most people would have been.
   ☐ b. Two fishermen found Elian about three miles from the Florida coast.
   ☐ c. Elian was still tied to the inner tube when he was found off the Florida coast.

2. From information in the article, you can predict that

   ☐ a. after hearing what happened to this group, more Cubans will try to get to Florida in small boats.
   ☐ b. after hearing about this group, other Cubans will be afraid of trying to escape to Florida in small boats.
   ☐ c. people in Florida will begin to build small boats so that they can take them to Cuba.

3. Elizabet and Lazaro are alike because

   ☐ a. they both survived the trip.
   ☐ b. both of them built the boat.
   ☐ c. they both died at sea.

4. At first, the fishermen thought Elian was a doll. Then they changed their minds. What was the cause of this change of mind?

   ☐ a. Elian called to them.
   ☐ b. Elian waved to them.
   ☐ c. Elian swam over to their boat.

5. Which paragraph provides information that supports your answer to question 4?

☐ a. paragraph 4

☐ b. paragraph 6

☐ c. paragraph 13

Score 4 points for each correct answer.

_____ **Total Score:** Critical Thinking

Enter your score for each activity. Add the scores together. Record your total score on the graph on page 115.

_____ Finding the Main Idea

_____ Recalling Facts

_____ Making Inferences

_____ Using Words

_____ Author's Approach

_____ Summarizing and Paraphrasing

_____ Critical Thinking

_____ **Total Score**

Personal Response

If you could ask the author of the article one question, what would it be?_____

_____

_____

Self-Assessment

I can't really understand how _____

_____

_____

Together Again After 50 Years

Ryang Han-sang was worried. He wondered how his mother was doing. He wondered about his younger brothers and sister too. For 50 years, Ryang had been separated from his family. He couldn't call them. He couldn't write them or visit them. He had no way of knowing whether they were alive or dead.

2   Ryang grew up in southern Korea. That's where his whole family had lived. But in 1950, when he was still a young man, war broke out between South Korea and North Korea. Ryang got stuck on the north side of the border, and he couldn't get back home. As the years went by, the two countries remained at war. People on one side were not allowed to have any contact with people on the other. So Ryang had no way to get in touch with his family. In time, he built a new life in North Korea. He got a job working for the North Korean government. But he never forgot his family in South Korea.

North Koreans wave from bus windows to South Koreans after the fifth reunion meeting of separated families had taken place.

3   Meanwhile Ryang's mother, Kim Ae-ran, didn't forget either. She missed her son terribly. Was he alive? Was he safe? Was he well? As the years dragged by, Kim Ae-ran couldn't stop thinking about him. Often she dreamed of him. But as she grew into an old woman, her hope faded. It looked as though she would go to her grave not knowing the fate of her oldest child.

4   Then, in 2000, something wonderful happened. The leaders of North and South Korea made a deal. They knew that thousands of families had been torn apart by the war. They decided to let a few of these families have reunions. One hundred North Koreans were picked. On August 15, 2000, these people were flown to South Korea. There they could spend three days visiting long-lost family members. To Ryang's joy, he was one of the ones picked to go.

5   When Ryang arrived in South Korea, he was taken to a hotel. Here the members of his family would be waiting for him. Sixty-nine-year-old Ryang looked around with excitement, and soon he saw his two brothers. Like Ryang, both were now in their 60s. His little sister had been just eight years old the last time Ryang saw her. She was now 58. But on this day, their ages did not matter. The years seemed to fall away as they stepped into each other's arms.

6 Ryang was thrilled to see his siblings, but most of all, he wanted to see his mother. When Ryang asked where she was, his brother gave him the bad news. Eighty-seven-year-old Kim Ae-ran was very sick. For three years she had been too weak to leave her home. Even though she lived just 40 minutes from the hotel, she was not well enough to make the trip.

7 Ryang had waited so long—he simply had to see his mother before he returned to North Korea. He asked officials if he could go to her house to visit her. They said no. North Korea and South Korea were still technically at war. Neither side trusted the other. So officials would not let Ryang travel freely. They told him he had to stay at the hotel. If the reunion couldn't take place there, then it couldn't take place at all.

8 Ryang felt awful. "If I don't see my mother, then it would have been better if I had not come to South Korea," he said bitterly.

9 He was allowed to make a phone call to her, but that just made him sadder. "I talked to her on the phone," he said, "and I couldn't stop crying."

10 Ryang was not the only one who was upset. Everyone who heard about his case thought it was unfair. Reporters wrote stories about it, and TV stations covered it. People everywhere thought that Ryang should be able to see his mother.

11 But time was running out. By August 18, Ryang didn't think he stood a chance. The next morning he had to return to North Korea. And officials still said he could not go to his mother's home.

12 Luckily, at the last minute someone thought of a new plan. Kim Ae-ran was too weak to travel, but she could be admitted to a hospital. That way everyone could be happy. Officials could still say that no meetings would take place in private homes. Yet Ryang would get to see his mother.

13 It took several hours to put the plan into action. At last, at 2:30 the next morning, Ryang, along with his brothers and sister, went to the hospital. When he stepped up to his mother's bedside, tears rolled down his cheeks.

14 "Ah, who is this?" cried Kim Ae-ran. Then she burst into tears and asked, "Why are you so late?"

15 "Forgive me, Mother, it's me," he said. "I am sorry for not sending my regards to you for a long time."

16 For the next half hour, the family talked and cried together, but all too soon it was time for Ryang to go. It was very hard to say goodbye. Ryang knew he might never see his mother again. But at least now he had some fresh memories of her. At least now he could give one last hug to the mother he had been missing for 50 years. ✿

A. Finding the Main Idea

One statement below tells the main idea of the article. One statement is too general, or too broad. The other statement explains only part of the article; it is too narrow. Label the statements using the following key:

M—Main Idea   B—Too Broad   N—Too Narrow

_____ 1. We may not know how much our families mean to us until we are separated from them. It is sad when we are not able to keep in touch with our parents, brothers, and sisters.

_____ 2. War in Korea separated a man from his family for 50 years. In 2000 he was thrilled when the governments of North and South Korea allowed him to see his family again on a short visit.

_____ 3. Even though Ryang Han-sang was happy to see his brothers and sister again, he was not satisfied until he visited his mother. After she was admitted to a hospital, he was able to see her there.

Score 4 points for each correct answer.

_____ **Total Score:** Finding the Main Idea

B. Recalling Facts

How well do you remember the facts in the article? Put an X in the box next to the answer that correctly completes each statement.

1. When North Korea and South Korea went to war, Ryang Han-sang was stuck in
☐ a. North Korea.
☐ b. South Korea.
☐ c. China.

2. After a few years apart from his family, Ryang Han-sang
☐ a. stopped thinking about them.
☐ b. got a job at a hospital.
☐ c. got a job with the government.

3. Ryang Han-sang's visit to his family lasted
☐ a. three days.
☐ b. three weeks.
☐ c. three months.

4. Ryang Han-sang's mother did not come to see him because she
☐ a. had forgotten him.
☐ b. was too weak.
☐ c. lived too far away.

Score 4 points for each correct answer.

_____ **Total Score:** Recalling Facts

C. Making Inferences

When you draw a conclusion that is not directly stated in the text, you are making an inference. Put an X in the box next to the statement that is a correct inference.

1.

☐ a. Life gets better for all citizens when their countries are at war.

☐ b. Sometimes governments care more about power than about the happiness of their people.

☐ c. Most people agree that family members in countries at war should not be allowed to contact each other.

2.

☐ a. Ryang Han-sang probably thinks that the visit with his family was a little too long.

☐ b. Ryang Han-sang probably hates people in the other part of Korea since his government is at war with them.

☐ c. There are other families separated by the war in Korea who probably hope that the governments will allow more visits.

Score 4 points for each correct answer.

_____ **Total Score:** Making Inferences

D. Using Words

Put an X in the box next to the definition below that is closest in meaning to the underlined word.

1. The prisoner has not had <u>contact</u> with the outside world for 20 years.

☐ a. one of the four seasons

☐ b. a bringing together

☐ c. separation

2. Family members from all over the United States come back home for our yearly <u>reunions</u>.

☐ a. get-togethers for people who are separated

☐ b. times for talking on the phone with friends

☐ c. pieces of mail, such as letters and postcards

3. Tyrone and all his <u>siblings</u> are tall, like their father.

☐ a. brothers and sisters

☐ b. aunts and uncles

☐ c. friends and neighbors

4. The countries have been <u>technically</u> at war for many years, even though they haven't really had any battles.

☐ a. never

☐ b. later

☐ c. officially

5. The customers complained <u>bitterly</u> when the store raised its prices.

☐ a. happily
☐ b. angrily
☐ c. kindly

6. I was pleased when my family and friends sent me their <u>regards</u> on my birthday.

☐ a. words of anger and disappointment
☐ b. worst fears
☐ c. messages of love and respect

Score 4 points for each correct answer.

_____ **Total Score:** Using Words

E. Author's Approach

Put an X in the box next to the correct answer.

1. The author uses the first sentence of the article to

☐ a. let readers know that Ryang Han-sang had a problem.
☐ b. describe Ryang Han-sang.
☐ c. describe Ryang Han-sang's family.

2. The author probably wrote this article in order to

☐ a. explain why North and South Korea were at war.
☐ b. tell how Ryang Han-sang met his family again.
☐ c. make readers stay away from North and South Korea.

3. The author tells this story mainly by

☐ a. describing events in time order.
☐ b. comparing different topics.
☐ c. using his or her imagination.

Score 4 points for each correct answer.

_____ **Total Score:** Author's Approach

F. Summarizing and Paraphrasing

Put an X in the box next to the correct answer.

1. Which summary says all the important things about the article?

☐ a. When war broke out in 1950, Ryang Han-sang was separated from the rest of his family. For 50 years his family missed him, but he was not allowed home.

☐ b. Ryang Han-sang had not seen his family in 50 years. When he visited South Korea, he saw his sister and brothers. At a hospital, he saw his mother too.

☐ c. Ryang Han-sang, who grew up in South Korea, was kept away from his family for 50 years by war. In 2000 he was allowed to visit his family, including his sick mother.

2. Which sentence means the same thing as the following sentence? "The years seemed to fall away as they stepped into each other's arms."

☐ a. When they hugged each other, all the years apart seemed to disappear.

☐ b. They touched each other and wished the years had not passed.

☐ c. Their arms touched as they stood beside each other, wishing this time would last forever.

Score 4 points for each correct answer.

_____ **Total Score:** Summarizing and Paraphrasing

G. Critical Thinking

Put an X in the box next to the correct answer.

1. Choose the statement below that states an opinion.

☐ a. Ryang Han-sang was about 19 years old in 1950.

☐ b. The North and South Korean governments were right to keep Ryang Han-sang and his family apart.

☐ c. Korean officials did not want Ryang Han-sang to meet his mother in her home.

2. Ryang Han-sang and his brothers are alike because they

☐ a. all worked for the government.

☐ b. all were stuck in North Korea when the war broke out.

☐ c. were all in their 60s at the time of Ryang's visit.

3. What was the cause of Kim Ae-ran's stay in the hospital?

☐ a. She went there so she could see Ryang.

☐ b. She was afraid she was dying and wanted doctors to look at her.

☐ c. She had trouble breathing and needed oxygen.

4. Which paragraph provides information that supports your answer to question 3?

☐ a. paragraph 9

☐ b. paragraph 10

☐ c. paragraph 12

5. Which lesson about life does this story teach?

☐ a. In many families, the members care about each other for their entire lives.

☐ b. You can always count on your government to do what is best for you.

☐ c. If you can't make a dream come true within a few years, you should probably give it up.

Score 4 points for each correct answer.

_____ **Total Score:** Critical Thinking

Enter your score for each activity. Add the scores together. Record your total score on the graph on page 115.

_____ Finding the Main Idea

_____ Recalling Facts

_____ Making Inferences

_____ Using Words

_____ Author's Approach

_____ Summarizing and Paraphrasing

_____ Critical Thinking

_____ **Total Score**

Personal Response

I know how Ryang Han-sang felt because _____

_____

_____

Self-Assessment

One of the things I did best when reading this article was

_____

_____

I believe I did this well because _____

_____

_____

Nightmare on a Plane

Jeanne Moore loved to travel. The 53-year-old schoolteacher had already seen much of the world. Now she was traveling through Asia. First she visited Nepal. She took a sightseeing trip to Mount Everest. Next she planned to see the famous Taj Mahal in India. On December 24, 1999, Moore boarded a plane for India. She expected a short flight. But as Moore later said, "I was on a two-hour trip that turned into a disaster."

2 The flight began in an ordinary way—nice and quiet. But after about an hour, Moore heard loud noises. "I saw food trays flying everywhere," she later said. She saw two men running down the aisle. They wore ski masks and carried guns. Then a chilling announcement came over the loudspeaker. "This plane has been hijacked."

3 Everyone knew what that meant. Someone had taken control of the plane away from the pilots. The plane would now fly anywhere the hijackers wanted to go.

Hostage survivor Jeanne Moore (center) hugs her daughters at the end of a news conference in Los Angeles.

4 In all, there were five hijackers. They had one demand. They wanted the leaders of India to release a man named Azhar from prison. The hijackers meant business. "They pointed guns and told people not to move," said Moore. "There was a clear understanding they would shoot." At times they said they would kill the passengers.

5 On the first day, they did kill a passenger. The victim was an Indian man. The other 155 passengers worried that they might be killed. Moore thought she might be. She was the only American on the plane. That made her nervous. Americans are often blamed for the world's problems. "I always felt the pressure of being an American," she said. Moore said she expected "the worst to happen to me."

6 During the first day, the hijackers forced the pilot to fly from place to place. They kept all the window shades pulled down so the people on board could not tell where they were. At last the plane landed in Afghanistan. For the next eight days, it did not move. In fact, the plane never left the ground again.

7 As the hours passed slowly by, Moore tried to figure out the hijackers, but she couldn't. At times they seemed nice. One hijacker sang and asked the passengers to join him. He even cracked jokes. The hijackers also handed out food. They asked everyone to pray together. But

Moore later said she suspected this was all part of their "mind games." She played a little mind game of her own. She talked for hours with a hijacker who spoke English. "I figured that the more we talked, the harder it would be for him to kill me," she said.

8   At other times the hijackers were brutal. Once a bug landed on Moore's arm. She turned her face to blow it off. Her sudden movement brought swift punishment. One of the hijackers smacked her on the head. "It is truly amazing that anyone can be so cruel," said Moore.

9   The passengers wanted this nightmare to end. But they feared a rescue attempt. They could imagine soldiers rushing at the plane with guns. If that happened, the passengers might be killed in the shooting. Moore pictured herself trapped with "bullets being sprayed and me in the middle."

10   It wasn't easy being held for so long on the plane. There was no fresh air. Some people had trouble breathing. The toilets overflowed. The odor in the cabin was foul. "Words cannot describe the smell," said Moore. Sometimes there was food, but sometimes there wasn't. It was very difficult to sleep. Moore slept only a couple of hours a day. That was partly her choice. If something big happened, she wanted to be awake and alert.

11   At one point, Moore definitely believed she was about to be killed. One of the hijackers asked her, "What do you call the box to keep a body?"

12   "I thought it was meant for me," Moore recalled. "I spelled the word, *coffin,* and wrote it on a piece of paper." She gave it to the hijacker and then waited for the end to come.

13   But the hijackers didn't kill her. She knew they could change their minds at any moment, so she stayed tense. "We were scared a lot," said Moore. "We never knew what was going to happen to us."

14   Meanwhile, the hijackers kept demanding that Azhar be released from prison. The leaders of India refused. On day five, the hijackers raised their demands. They wanted 36 prisoners to be released. They also demanded 200 million dollars. The next day, they dropped the demand for money. At last, on day eight, the two sides made a deal. India would free Azhar and two other prisoners. In return the hijackers would let the hostages go.

15   The details were soon worked out. A few hours later, an official stepped onto the plane. He looked at the passengers and said, "It's over."

16   "It was eerily quiet in the cabin," Moore recalled. "I was grateful that we were going out with a whimper and not a bang."

17   Jeanne Moore was later asked if she planned to travel again. She thought for a moment about the hijackers. Then she nodded. She said, "If you change your life, then they win even more." 🎗

A. Finding the Main Idea

One statement below tells the main idea of the article. One statement is too general, or too broad. The other statement explains only part of the article; it is too narrow. Label the statements using the following key:

M—Main Idea   **B—Too Broad**   **N—Too Narrow**

_____ 1. Jeanne Moore, a passenger on a flight to India, was frightened when hijackers took over the plane. She was afraid that they would kill her because she was an American.

_____ 2. Hijackers took over a plane. They said they would keep the plane and its passengers until Indian leaders released a man from prison. Days later a deal was made, and the hijackers let the passengers go.

_____ 3. When hijackers take over a plane, an ordinary journey can become a nightmare. Usually, the hijackers make demands that are hard to meet. Sometimes leaders give in to demands, and sometimes they resist.

Score 4 points for each correct answer.

_____ **Total Score:** Finding the Main Idea

B. Recalling Facts

How well do you remember the facts in the article? Put an X in the box next to the answer that correctly completes each statement.

1. The plane was supposed to fly to
☐ a. Nepal.
☐ b. India.
☐ c. the United States.

2. The hijackers took the plane to
☐ a. Afghanistan.
☐ b. India.
☐ c. England.

3. In addition to demanding that Azhar be released, the hijackers wanted
☐ a. two million dollars and the release of 36 million prisoners.
☐ b. 36 million dollars and the release of 200 prisoners.
☐ c. 200 million dollars and the release of 36 prisoners.

4. The passengers were let go after
☐ a. two days.
☐ b. eight days.
☐ c. 36 days.

Score 4 points for each correct answer.

_____ **Total Score:** Recalling Facts

C. Making Inferences

When you draw a conclusion that is not directly stated in the text, you are making an inference. Put an X in the box next to the statement that is a correct inference.

1.

☐ a. After a while, the hijackers and the passengers became good friends.

☐ b. It is possible that hostages can be killed when people try to rescue them.

☐ c. If hijackers act pleasant, you can be sure they will never hurt their hostages.

2.

☐ a. What the hijackers wanted most was the release of Azhar.

☐ b. The restrooms on the plane were cleaned out every day.

☐ c. Indian officials did not care about the safety of the hostages.

Score 4 points for each correct answer.

_____ **Total Score:** Making Inferences

D. Using Words

Put an X in the box next to the definition below that is closest in meaning to the underlined word.

1. The storm was a <u>disaster</u> for the families who lost their homes.

☐ a. an event that brings happiness and joy

☐ b. an event that brings sadness or suffering

☐ c. an event that happened recently

2. One of the robbers was <u>brutal</u>, but the other seemed much kinder.

☐ a. cruel

☐ b. silly

☐ c. weak

3. He made a face when he smelled the <u>foul</u> odor that came from the bag of old garbage.

☐ a. pleasant

☐ b. sweet

☐ c. disgusting

4. It is hard to stay <u>alert</u> when you haven't had much sleep for days.

☐ a. ready for action

☐ b. very sleepy

☐ c. tired and grumpy

5. The <u>hostages</u> tried to escape when the guards were not looking.

☐ a. people holding others against their will
☐ b. people held prisoner until demands are met
☐ c. people remembering an important event from the past

6. Jenny shivered with a strange fear when dark clouds floated <u>eerily</u> over the moon and blocked its light.

☐ a. loudly
☐ b. brightly
☐ c. weirdly

Score 4 points for each correct answer.

_____ **Total Score:** Using Words

E. Author's Approach

Put an X in the box next to the correct answer.

1. What is the author's purpose in writing this article?

☐ a. to make the reader afraid to travel anywhere
☐ b. to tell the reader about a scary journey
☐ c. to entertain with a funny story

2. From the statements below, choose the one that you believe the author would agree with.

☐ a. Jeanne Moore would be foolish ever to fly again.
☐ b. Indian officials didn't care that hijackers took over the plane.
☐ c. The hijackers were cruel to the passengers.

3. Choose the statement below that is the weakest argument for hijacking a plane.

☐ a. It can make you famous.
☐ b. It can get you killed.
☐ c. You may get what you were asking for.

Score 4 points for each correct answer.

_____ **Total Score:** Author's Approach

F. Summarizing and Paraphrasing

Put an X in the box next to the correct answer.

1. Which summary says all the important things about the article?

☐ a. Hijackers who took over a plane were cruel to the passengers. They often said that the passengers might be killed. They hit passengers and even killed one.

☐ b. After hijackers took over a plane, they made many demands. The demands kept changing over several days. Officials gave in to some of the demands.

☐ c. In December 1999, hijackers took over a plane and demanded the release of a prisoner. They kept 155 passengers as hostages. Finally, Indian officials made a deal, and the surviving hostages were let go.

2. Which sentence means the same thing as the following sentence? "I was grateful that we were going out with a whimper and not a bang."

☐ a. I was thankful that things were ending peacefully.

☐ b. I was surprised that everyone was whimpering instead of punishing the hijackers.

☐ c. Even though I felt sad about what had happened, I was glad that the hijacking was finally over.

Score 4 points for each correct answer.

_____ **Total Score:** Summarizing and Paraphrasing

G. Critical Thinking

Put an X in the box next to the correct answer.

1. Choose the statement below that states an opinion.

☐ a. The passengers understood that the hijackers were willing to shoot them.

☐ b. The passengers should have tried to fight the hijackers.

☐ c. At least one hijacker spoke English.

2. From information in the article, you can predict that

☐ a. many of the passengers will be nervous about traveling by plane in the future.

☐ b. no one will ever try to hijack a plane in India again.

☐ c. people carrying ski masks or any other ski clothing will not be allowed to board any planes in the future.

3. What was the effect of Jeanne Moore's sudden move to blow away a bug that had landed on her?

☐ a. The hijackers killed one passenger.

☐ b. One hijacker asked her how to spell a word that meant "a box to keep a body."

☐ c. A hijacker hit Moore in the head.

4. Which paragraph provides information that supports your answer to question 3?

☐ a. paragraph 7

☐ b. paragraph 8

☐ c. paragraph 11

5. Which lesson about life does this story teach?

☐ a. Everything always turns out well for everyone in the end.

☐ b. If you are friendly, you can be sure people will be kind to you.

☐ c. You shouldn't let fear rule your life.

Score 4 points for each correct answer.

_____ **Total Score:** Critical Thinking

Enter your score for each activity. Add the scores together. Record your total score on the graph on page 115.

_____ Finding the Main Idea

_____ Recalling Facts

_____ Making Inferences

_____ Using Words

_____ Author's Approach

_____ Summarizing and Paraphrasing

_____ Critical Thinking

_____ **Total Score**

Personal Response

Would you tell other students to read this article? Explain.

_____

_____

_____

Self-Assessment

One good question about this article that was not asked

would be "_____

_____

_____?"

Gone in an Instant

Every year the students looked forward to the trip. It was the highlight of the year for tenth graders at the Strathcona-Tweedsmuir School, known as STS, in Alberta, Canada. They went to Glacier National Park for four days of skiing. The trip is a long tradition at STS. This private school teaches all its students to love the outdoors. "This program is at the heart of who we are and how we educate," said a school official. Even first graders sleep in tents for a weekend.

2 Skiing in the park has its risks. Avalanches often sweep down the high slopes. (Avalanches are very large blocks of snow that break off and plunge down the side of a mountain, burying everything in their path.) On January 20, 2003, an avalanche killed seven people. That was less than two weeks before the STS trip began.

3 The trip's three adult leaders had plenty of experience. They knew the risks. They would be careful. The 14 students, too, had studied avalanches. They knew the danger signs. But just in case, all members of

Students from Strathcona-Tweedsmuir School mourn the loss of a fellow student who died in an avalanche at Glacier National Park.

the group carried shovels and wore beacons. The beacons are devices that send out beeping signals. If the wearers were trapped under snow, the beeps would help rescuers find them. "They were as prepared as they could have been," said an STS official.

4 The trip began on February 1. The group drove to a part of the park known as Rogers Pass. They left their vans and skied to a log cabin. The students did some tests to check snow conditions. They also compared the snow that fell in the night with snow already on the ground. Each layer of snow is a little different.

5 The next morning the group skied to the visitor center. Andrew Nicholson, one of the group's leaders, talked with officials there. Nicholson wanted to know what the weather would be like. He also wanted to know if there was much danger of an avalanche. The officials said that an avalanche was unlikely in the areas where the students planned to ski. But higher up, the danger was greater. There, they said, the danger of an avalanche was very possible. If an avalanche did start high above the STS group, it could mean trouble. There was nothing on the mountain to stop a large slab of sliding snow. So the trip was a risk. But the group agreed to chance it. As one student later said, "The risk is part of the reward."

6 At 9:30 A.M., the adults and the students headed up Balu Pass Trail. They moved in groups of two. A recent

snowfall had dropped two feet of fresh snow on the ground. The temperature was near 30 degrees. The wind was gentle. It looked like a great day for skiing.

7   Meanwhile, 300 feet above them, two other skiers had stopped for a rest. Rich Marshall and his wife, Abby Watkins, were standing near some trees at 5,500 feet. They watched the STS skiers move up the trail. It was 11:45 A.M. All at once, there was a loud crack. Marshall looked across the valley. On a slope far above the trail, a huge chunk of snow gave way. It swept down the mountain, heading straight for the STS skiers. "Avalanche! Avalanche! Avalanche!" Marshall yelled.

8   This was no ordinary snow slide—it was huge. First the top layer of snow began to move. If that had been all that had happened, it would have been all right. Some light powder would have dusted the skiers. But several lower layers also gave way. As a result, a massive slab of snow slid down the mountain. It was about 850 yards wide. It was strong enough to snap trees like matchsticks.

9   Marshall and Watkins were far enough away to be safe, but the STS skiers were not. The avalanche plowed right into them. One student who lived through it recalled seeing a "wall of snow." Then it was just "blackness."

10   Marshall and Watkins witnessed the whole disaster. They wanted to help, but they had to wait for the snow to settle. Then they rushed to the rescue. Marshall spotted an arm poking out of the snow. It was Andrew

Nicholson's. Marshall made sure Nicholson was alive and able to dig himself out. Then Marshall and Watkins moved on, looking for others.

11   "We saw just about everyone was buried," said Watkins. She and Marshall listened for beeps from the skiers' beacons. Then they began to dig. Each time they found a person, they made sure he or she could breathe. Then they moved on. Officials believe Marshall and Watkins saved at least five lives.

12   Once Nicholson dug himself out, he joined in the effort. He also used his cell phone to call for help. Within 40 minutes, 10 rescuers were on the scene. More came soon afterwards. In all, three adults and seven students lived through the avalanche. Among them, the worst injury was a broken ankle.

13   But not everyone made it out alive. The snow had knocked some of the skiers more than 200 yards down the trail. They could not be found in time. Seven students—six boys and one girl—died. Some of them were found buried under nine feet of snow.

14   Eric Dafoe, a park official, said that such a big avalanche is rare in Rogers Pass. When one does happen, it is usually during a snowstorm "when no one is around." But this time there were people in the pass. The STS students, Dafoe said sadly, "were just in the wrong place at the wrong time."

A. Finding the Main Idea

One statement below tells the main idea of the article. One statement is too general, or too broad. The other statement explains only part of the article; it is too narrow. Label the statements using the following key:

M—Main Idea   **B—Too Broad**   **N—Too Narrow**

_____ 1. Students on a class skiing trip in Glacier National Park were buried by an avalanche. Though rescuers began to look for them right away, seven students died.

_____ 2. Students from STS were prepared for a possible avalanche in Glacier National Park. They were wearing beacons that sent out beeping signals. If the need arose, rescuers could follow the beeps to find them.

_____ 3. No one expects to have to deal with a tragedy. But it is important to be ready for one anyway. That is especially true if you are going skiing in the mountains with a group of students.

Score 4 points for each correct answer.

_____ **Total Score:** Finding the Main Idea

B. Recalling Facts

How well do you remember the facts in the article? Put an X in the box next to the answer that correctly completes each statement.

1. The STS skiing trip began on
   ☐ a. March 30, 2002.
   ☐ b. February 22, 2000.
   ☐ c. February 1, 2003.

2. Rich Marshall and Abby Watkins were shocked when they saw
   ☐ a. the students leave their vans and ski to a log cabin.
   ☐ b. a heavy snowfall begin just as the students began their trip.
   ☐ c. a huge slab of snow head toward the students.

3. Marshall and Watkins were able to find Andrew Nicholson when they
   ☐ a. heard him shouting from under a pile of snow.
   ☐ b. saw his arm poking out of the snow.
   ☐ c. heard the beeping of his beacon.

4. The avalanche knocked some of the students as much as
   ☐ a. nine feet down the trail.
   ☐ b. 200 yards down the trail.
   ☐ c. 5,000 yards down the trail.

Score 4 points for each correct answer.

_____ **Total Score:** Recalling Facts

C. Making Inferences

When you draw a conclusion that is not directly stated in the text, you are making an inference. Put an X in the box next to the statement that is a correct inference.

1.

☐ a. Students didn't have much time to get away from the wall of snow that came at them.

☐ b. If you know the warning signs for an avalanche, you will never be caught in one.

☐ c. If the students had known that an avalanche was possible, none of them would have gone on the trip.

2.

☐ a. Park guides know exactly when avalanches will happen in Glacier National Park.

☐ b. It would have been easy to find all the students even without their beacons.

☐ c. Marshall and Watkins were willing to spend time and effort to rescue strangers.

Score 4 points for each correct answer.

_____ **Total Score:** Making Inferences

D. Using Words

Put an X in the box next to the definition below that is closest in meaning to the underlined word.

1. Most students looked forward to the class trip to the county fair as the <u>highlight</u> of the school year.

☐ a. the most important part of something
☐ b. something to be feared or dreaded
☐ c. a time for being alone and thinking deeply

2. A big turkey dinner has always been a Thanksgiving <u>tradition</u> in our family.

☐ a. an event that happens only once and never happens again

☐ b. a custom that is handed down from one group of people to another for many years

☐ c. a series of events that come as a surprise to the people who experience them

3. These simple <u>devices</u> will turn the lights on in your home at the same time every day.

☐ a. things that decorate a room
☐ b. rules to a game or sport
☐ c. things made to do a special task

4. Workers cut the kitchen counter from a <u>slab</u> of marble.

☐ a. a flat, wide, thick piece of something
☐ b. a small, round, piece of wood
☐ c. a long, thin metal pipe

5. When we were little, we rode our sleds down the <u>slope</u> in our back yard.

☐ a. outdoor building for storing garden tools
☐ b. line of bushes and other plants
☐ c. land that slants up or down

6. It took four men to move the <u>massive</u> sofa into place.

☐ a. small and light
☐ b. large and heavy
☐ c. quick and strong

Score 4 points for each correct answer.

_____ **Total Score:** Using Words

E. Author's Approach

Put an X in the box next to the correct answer.

1. What is the author's purpose in writing this article?

☐ a. to tell the story of an unlucky ski trip
☐ b. to explain how an avalanche begins
☐ c. to describe what it feels like to ski in Glacier National Park

2. From the statements below, choose the one that you believe the author would agree with.

☐ a. This was the first avalanche that ever happened in Rogers Pass.
☐ b. The adults in the ski party should have done a better job of preparing the students for an avalanche.
☐ c. The STS students were victims of bad luck that day.

3. The author tells this story mainly by

☐ a. describing events in the order they happened.
☐ b. comparing and contrasting different topics.
☐ c. using his or her imagination to guess what might have happened.

Score 4 points for each correct answer.

_____ **Total Score:** Author's Approach

F. Summarizing and Paraphrasing

Put an X in the box next to the correct answer.

1. Which summary says all the important things about the article?

☐ a. On the day that 14 students and their three adult leaders headed up Balu Pass in Glacier National Park, there was a light wind. The weather looked fine for skiing.

☐ b. At STS in Alberta, Canada, students are taught to love nature. Students of all ages have many chances to enjoy outdoor experiences such as camping and skiing.

☐ c. In 2003 a surprise avalanche killed seven students on a school ski trip in Glacier National Park. Seven students and three adults were rescued after being buried under several feet of snow.

2. Which sentence means the same thing as the following sentence about the wall of snow that buried the students? "It was strong enough to snap trees like matchsticks."

☐ a. It was weaker than most avalanches.
☐ b. It was so strong that it could easily snap trees.
☐ c. The trees that snapped were small.

Score 4 points for each correct answer.

_____ **Total Score:** Summarizing and Paraphrasing

G. Critical Thinking

Put an X in the box next to the correct answer.

1. Choose the statement below that states a fact.

☐ a. The slab of snow that buried the students was about 850 yards wide.
☐ b. Park officials should give away beacons to everyone who wants to ski in the parks.
☐ c. Anyone could have done at least as good a job as Marshall and Watkins did in rescuing the students.

2. From information in the article, you can predict that

☐ a. STS will no longer try to teach its students to love the outdoors.
☐ b. no one will ever ski in Glacier National Park again.
☐ c. skiers will continue to wear beacons.

3. Rich Marshall and Andrew Nicholson are different because

☐ a. only Nicholson helped rescue the students.
☐ b. only Nicholson was one of the group's adult leaders.
☐ c. only Marshall made a cell phone call for help.

4. What was the effect of the lower snow layers' sliding down the mountain along with the upper layers?

☐ a. The avalanche was bigger and stronger than most.
☐ b. Light powder dusted the skiers, but nothing else happened.
☐ c. The students learned that each layer of snow is a little different.

5. How is this STS skiing trip an example of a fateful journey?

☐ a. People learned that beacons were useless.

☐ b. Seven students lost their lives on the trip.

☐ c. Marshall and Watkins saw the students heading up the mountain.

Score 4 points for each correct answer.

_____ **Total Score:** Critical Thinking

Enter your score for each activity. Add the scores together. Record your total score on the graph on page 115.

_____ Finding the Main Idea

_____ Recalling Facts

_____ Making Inferences

_____ Using Words

_____ Author's Approach

_____ Summarizing and Paraphrasing

_____ Critical Thinking

_____ **Total Score**

Personal Response

Why do you think Marshall and Watkins moved on so quickly once they had made sure each student could breathe?_____

_____

_____

Self-Assessment

From reading this article, I have learned_____

_____

_____

Compare and Contrast

Pick two stories in Unit Three about journeys that were affected by actions of the leaders of one or more countries. Use information from the stories to fill in this chart.

Title	Who was traveling?	Which country or countries were involved?	How did the leaders of the countries help or hurt the travelers?

Which of the places mentioned in the stories would you like to visit? Why? _____

_____

_____

Comprehension and Critical Thinking Progress Graph

Directions: Write your score for each lesson in the box under the number of the lesson.
Then put a small X on the line directly above the number of the lesson and across from
the score you earned. Chart your progress by drawing a line to connect the Xs.

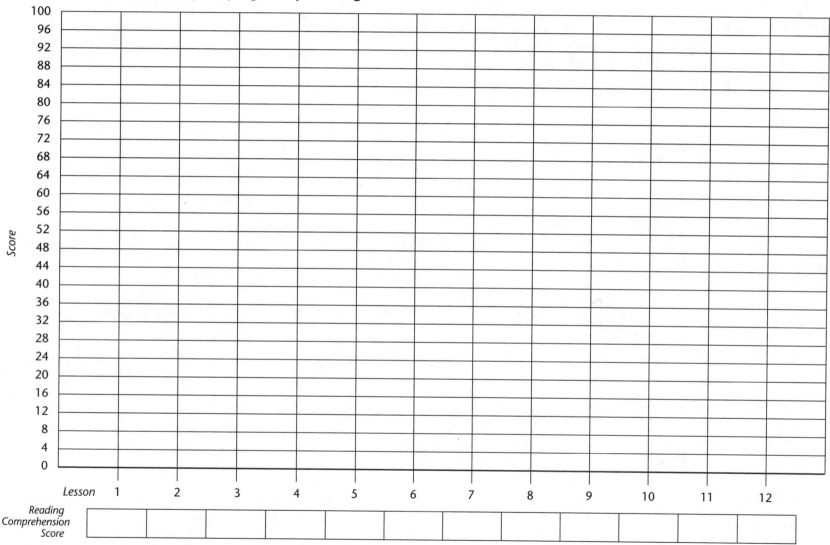

Photo Credits

Cover Galen Rowell/CORBIS; **3–4** NASA; **13** Jonathan Bursnall/Latin Focus.com; **14** AP/Wide World Photos; **22** Jonathan Bursnall/Latin Focus.com; **30** Mark Pepper/Marinepics; **38** Bettmann/CORBIS; **47** Gary Horlor; **48** Jorgos Tsambikakis/Reuters News Picture Service Photo; **56** Gary Horlor; **64** AP/Wide World Photos; **72** Richard H. Johnston/Getty Images; **81, 82, 90, 98** AP/Wide World Photos; **106** Patrick Price/Reuters News Picture Service Photo.